P9-DOD-111

MURDER IN
THE FOURTH ESTATE

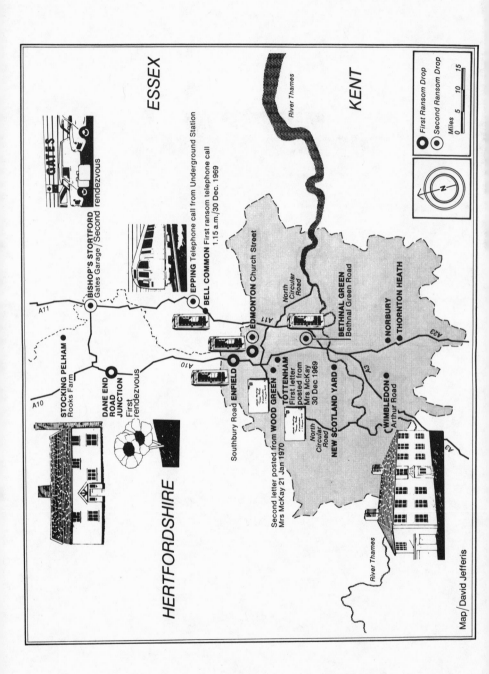

ESSEX

KENT

River Thames

First Ransom Drop
Second Ransom Drop
Miles
0   5   10   15

N

GATES

BISHOP'S STORTFORD
Gates Garage/Second rendezvous

EPPING Telephone call from Underground Station
BELL COMMON First ransom telephone call
1.15 a.m./30 Dec. 1969

EDMONTON Church Street

North
Circular
Road

BETHNAL GREEN
Bethnal Green Road

NORBURY
THORNTON HEATH

A11

STOCKING PELHAM
Rooks Farm

DANE END
ROAD
JUNCTION
First
rendezvous

A10

Southbury Road WOOD GREEN ENFIELD

TOTTENHAM
First letter
posted from
Mrs McKay
30 Dec 1969

A10

North
Circular
Road

NEW SCOTLAND YARD

A3

WIMBLEDON
Arthur Road

A23

Second letter posted from WOOD GREEN
Mrs McKay 21 Jan 1970

HERTFORDSHIRE

River Thames

A3

Map/David Jefferis

MURDER IN THE FOURTH ESTATE

by *Peter Deeley*
and *Christopher Walker*

McGraw-Hill Book Company
New York   St. Louis   San Francisco

We acknowledge with thanks permission for use of the
photographs in the picture section, as follows:
 Page 1 (top and bottom), page 2 (top and bottom),
page 3 (top and bottom), pages 4 and 5, page 7 (top),
Copyright © The Press Association Ltd., 85 Fleet Street,
London EC4, England. The artist's impressions of Arthur
and Nizam Hosein on Page 7 were drawn by David Jefferis.
 Page 6 (top and bottom), page 7 (bottom), page 8 (top
and bottom), photographs by *London Daily Express—
Pictorial Parade.*

Copyright © 1971 by Peter Deeley and Christopher Walker.
All rights reserved.
Printed in the United States of America.
No part of this publication may
be reproduced, stored in a retrieval
system, or transmitted,
in any form or by any means,
electronic, mechanical, photocopying,
recording or otherwise, without the prior written permission
of the publisher.

First edition in the United States of America 1973
123456789BPBP79876543
First printed in Great Britain by Victor Gollancz Ltd.
Library of Congress Cataloging in Publication Data

Deeley, Peter.
 Murder in the fourth estate.

 1. Kidnapping—Wimbledon, Eng.—Case studies.
2. Murder—Wimbledon, Eng.—Case studies. I. Walker,
Christopher, joint author. II. Title.
HV6604.E52M33 1973 364.1'523 72-10060
ISBN 0-07-016214-X

Contents

1
SPINNING THE WEB

WIMBLEDON IS ONE of those English suburbs in which every brick seems to have been laid with the rich in mind. Situated only seven miles from the centre of London, it gives the impression of having been designed by a computer programmed only with the needs of affluent commuters. Like so many dormitory towns, it is a place where very little out of the ordinary happens—and what does tends to be despressingly predictable. Every morning the men leave by train and car to work in London. By the time they return at night, most have little energy or enthusiasm to create any local life. Every summer, Wimbledon becomes the focus of the world's attention for the brief duration of the tennis championships. But the television cameras and the pressmen never stray much farther than the Centre Court. In winter, there is always a Christmas pantomime at the local theatre; more often than not it seems to be *Jack and the Beanstalk*.

The town is partitioned into two clearly definable sections, rather in the way that nineteenth century town houses were built with servants' quarters. The lower end, with the railway station, light industry, and the greyhound stadium is for those who have not yet made it; the upper end, with its green wooded common, expensive eating houses, and large mansions is unquestionably for those who have. The upper end, which is close to the spacious common, is commonly referred to as the "village." This is because the shops along the High Street have been built mostly in country style, with small windows and a rather self-conscious quaintness. It is a place where a high price is paid for privacy, and it is not hard to understand why it has so long been one of the most sought after residential districts on the fringes of London.

Arthur Road is no different from the many other roads which run off from the "village" High Street: wide, with a neatly trimmed grass verge, trees, and a number of large mansions, all separated by gardens and approached by way of small drives. Halfway down on the left hand side is St. Mary's Church, a pleasant, tidy building with a healthy congregation of predominantly middle-aged residents. Opposite the church is the Old Rectory, lived in by the vicar and his wife, and next to that number 20 Arthur Road, St. Mary House.

As the architect no doubt intended, the house conveys an immediate feeling of solid affluence. It is a large, red-brick mansion built in mock-georgian style with attractive white windows and a majestic-looking front door. The house stands back some ten yards from the road, and has an asphalt driveway running past the front door with entrances at either end of a tall fence which screens the house from the road. On the left-hand side of the building is a double garage, and behind that a neat garden. Today, anyone who paid less than £30,000 for it would have picked up a bargain.

Alick and Muriel McKay paid under £20,000 for St. Mary House when they bought it in 1958. For the rugged-faced Australian newspaper executive who had recently arrived in Britain from his native Adelaide, it was an important symbol of prestige. Later, whenever the couple felt the inevitable pangs of homesickness, the house was to provide a significant root.

Alick McKay was born in Adelaide, South Australia, on 5th August, 1909. His father was a master mariner, captain of a small coastal steamer which made a regular journey between Spencer's Gulf and St. Vincent Gulf on the neighbouring seaboard. It was a job of which George McKay was intensely proud, and his son had to resist strong family pressure to follow in his footsteps. In the early years of this century, Adelaide was a town acutely aware of the social differences, having inherited and magnified many of the snobbish attitudes of Victorian Britain. This was something of a disadvantage for Alick, whose family could only afford to have him state-educated at Trebarton High School.

Muriel McKay, then Muriel Searcy, was five years younger than her husband. She was also born in Adelaide on 4th February, 1914. Her father was an executive in the motor industry, which was in those early days still struggling to find its feet. With his money, she was educated at one of the town's smarter private schools.

The difference in educational background was the only evident barrier between the couple, who met and fell in love at a local Sunday school when Muriel was only fifteen years old. But their feelings for each other were strong enough to overcome the social differences, and they were married four years later. By this time Alick had embarked on his career. His first introduction to the newspaper world came through Muriel's brother, who was advertising manager of the *Adelaide News*. The paper was part of News Ltd., the group owned by Sir Keith Murdoch, who was then well on his way to becoming Australia's most powerful press baron. It was in 1933 that Alick first formed a link with the Murdoch family which was eventually to have disastrous consequences. In that year, he joined News Ltd. in Adelaide. He went straight into the management side of the Press—and over the next two decades, his ambition took him far inside the organisation. He was put in charge of both the Melbourne and Sydney offices, and given other influential posts.

In 1952, he left Murdoch to become general manager of Argus and Australasian Ltd., then owned by the London *Daily Mirror*, the world's most successful tabloid newspaper. In 1957 came promotion in the form of an offer from the parent group, and—to his surprise as much as everyone else's—Alick McKay found himself on the way to London to take up a new post as advertisement director of Daily Mirror Newspapers. The appointment of this relatively unknown Australian caused a stir in Fleet Street, where it had been confidently predicted that the much sought-after job would automatically go to someone already familiar with the territory. To begin with, Alick McKay was treated with a certain amount of suspicion and resentment, but this soon gave way to liking and respect.

On arriving in London, the McKays began house-hunting. Before long they found St. Mary House. Once they had settled there, life for them took on a fairly regular pattern for the next few years. Together they made a handsome couple. Alick was tall, with an open face, a marked Australian accent and a liking for the good things of life. Like all ambitious men, he had a taste for power. His wife was dedicated to furthering his career, and soon made a name for herself as a hostess. She was a strikingly attractive woman, about five feet nine inches tall, with stylish dark hair and green eyes. Always warm and friendly, she charmed people with her straightforwardness and simplicity—rare attributes among wives of leading British businessmen and politicians. "She was," said one close friend, "one of the most unaffected women I have ever met."

The MacKays had three children, two daughters and a son. The daughters, Diane and Jennifer, both married and settled in England. Diane, who was closest to her mother, married David Dyer, a tough, energetic English businessman who made a successful career working for Wilkinson, the razor blade manufacturers. Jennifer, the quieter of the two girls, married Ian Burgess, an affable, easy-going property dealer and horse breeder. The son, Ian, who was only fourteen when the family first arrived in England, eventually went back to Australia and followed his father into the advertising side of newspapers.

After her family had grown up and left home, Muriel McKay settled happily into the routine existence of a well-off, upper-middle-class housewife. She was fond of fashionable clothes, and spent a considerable amount of money on them. She painted the odd still-life and hung it up around the house. She was a member of the local Wives' Fellowship, among other organizations, and was a regular churchgoer and a keen supporter of the Wimbledon Tory Party. The M.P. for the constituency was Sir Cyril Black, well known for his one-man stand against the permissive society. He described Mrs. McKay as "a good conservative."

Throughout the early sixties, her husband's influence was increasing. Already a director and board member of Daily Mirror Newspapers, his responsibilities grew as various magazine and publishing companies were added to the Mirror empire. To meet the expansion, a parent group called the International Publishing Corporation (IPC) was created in 1963, and McKay was made advertisement director. With each new acquisition, he was given control of the advertising side, and before long his job was to cover most of the women's magazines in the country. In addition, in 1962 he had been appointed chairman of George Newnes, the old established magazine, encyclopaedia and publishing company. Apart from his job, he could boast a formidable list of spare time activities. He was chairman of the Victoria Promotions Committee, which promoted the State of Victoria in the United Kingdom. He was also chairman of the International Export Council and the Heart Foundation Appeals Committee. Alick McKay was a great man for formal occasions. In the 1965 Honours List, under Harold Wilson's new Labour Goverment, he was awarded the CBE for services to exporting.

By this time, the McKays' social circle included men like Cecil King, Hugh Cudlipp, Lord Robens (then Chairman of the National Coal Board) and a variety of high ranking diplomatic officials from Australia House. As an influential voice in the fourth estate and its related fields, Alick McKay had arrived. This fact, of which he and his family were well aware, was to have its relevance in the events which follow.

In 1966, the pace of McKay's business and social life took its toll, and he suffered a mild heart attack. This was followed by a more serious attack a year later, and for a time he had to cut down his responsibilities at IPC. Early in 1968, the company's chairman, Cecil King, sent him off on a long boat-trip to Australia, hoping that the rest would help him recuperate. But McKay's luck was out, and he fell against a bollard on the journey and injured his leg. When he returned to England, this developed into another thrombosis. McKay received a number of severe warnings from his doctor, and as a result let it be known inside the IPC hierarchy that because of ill health, he would be retiring in 1969 at the age of sixty. But his constitution proved tougher than expected, and he made a rapid recovery. In the summer of 1969, a friend recalls meeting McKay at a formal dinner in London: "Alick was very excited because he had just come back from the doctor. He ran up three flights of stairs to the surgery, pulled open his dress shirt and ordered the doctor to listen to his heart. Apparently there was hardly a murmur."

Back to health, Alick was reluctant to disappear into the obscurity of retirement, or to return to his native Australia as he had originally planned. Psychologically at least, he was in the market for another job. Although Muriel, now aged fifty-five, put no barriers in his way, it was no secret that she would have preferred Alick to settle for a quieter life. She was also looking forward to going back more often to her homeland.

By complete coincidence, a fellow Australian and friend of the McKays had arrived in London the previous year. He was Rupert Murdoch, the ambitious son of Sir Keith Murdoch, McKay's first employer. Already, in the short period he had been in Fleet Street, he had made a mark similar in proportion to that of the other two powerful Commonwealth press barons of the twentieth century, Lord Beaverbrook and Lord Thomson. When Sir Keith died in 1954, it had been confidently expected that he would leave the whole of his vast newspaper empire to his son. Instead, he left Rupert, who was then twenty-two, just a 15 per cent share in an insignificant Adelaide afternoon paper. But this only served to harden Rupert's determination. A former student at Oxford University (where he took a third class degree in Philosophy, Politics and Economics), Murdoch trained briefly as a sub editor on the London *Daily Express.* He used the Adelaide paper as a base for a number of daring takeovers in the heart of Australia's established press world. Having bought the ailing Sydney *Sunday Mirror,* and later the Sydney *Daily Mirror,* he then started up a chain of highly profitable suburban papers.

To readers of the British satirical magazine *Private Eye,* Murdoch has always been known rather unflatteringly as the "Dirty Digger." The name was coined because many of his Australian papers have an unrivalled reputation for publishing sensation, sex, and scandal. This is particularly true of the *Truth* series, which prints separate editions in Brisbane, Adelaide, and Melbourne. A typical front page story from the Melbourne *Truth* begins, "A forty-five-year-old man has been found guilty of DRUGGING BEER in an ATTEMPT TO SEDUCE his twenty-year-old daughter-in-law. The woman has told of finding CAPSULES in a glass of beer poured by her father-in-law, who visited her when she was ALONE in her home. She has also told of her father-in-law's suggestion that they should go together to the BEDROOM." To British readers, the crudeness of the style seems like a caricature. In fact, that is exactly how the paper is written—including the strategic words set in capital letters, just in case any innocents may have missed the nuance of what is being reported.

But Murdoch, a one-time member of the Oxford University Labour Club, has a mind made up of a curious contradiction of attitudes. Not all his papers indulge in such lurid material. In 1964, he conceived the idea of starting Australia's first national daily paper—a bold notion in such a huge and scattered continent. The paper, called the *Australian*, is now generally rated as the best quality daily in the country.

Despite his success at home, Murdoch still hankered after recognition in Britain. For journalists all over the world, Fleet Street is the Mecca, and like so many of his fellow Australians, Murdoch was anxious to find a way of getting a foothold there. His chance came sooner than expected. Late in 1968, the News of the World Organisation, publishers of the world's largest-selling newspaper (with a circulation of over six million every Sunday), was fighting tooth and nail to ward off an unwanted takeover bid from Pergamon Press, the company owned by the controversial millionaire and socialist M.P., Robert Maxwell.

In Britain, the *News of the World* had a reputation similar to that of some of Murdoch's papers in Australia. It specialised in pin-ups, scandalous memoirs, exposés, and court stories of the "vicar and the choir boy" variety. To its chairman, Sir William Carr, at that time very ill in hospital, Murdoch—the bright young boy from down under—appeared the obvious ally against Maxwell.

The fight between Maxwell and the *News of the World* lasted for two months, and cost Maxwell £200,000 in Merchant Banker's fees alone. It was one of the most acrimonious the City has seen. It began on 16th October, 1968, when Pergamon Press, the scientific publishing house which Maxwell had founded, bid £26.7 million for the N.O.W. The bid was backed by 26 per cent of the shares, which had been sold secretly to Maxwell in Paris by one of the lesser-known family shareholders. The traditionally Tory Carr family could not abide the idea of selling out to a socialist, especially one like Robert Maxwell, who had been a refugee from Eastern Europe. On the Sunday following the Pergamon bid, the *News of the World* carried a lengthy front page diatribe written by the editor, Stafford Somerfield. "We are having a little local difficulty," it began. The paper shared the English habit of disliking foreigners, and the article contained one memorable paragraph which well illustrated the viciousness of the take-over battle: "It would not be a good thing for Mr. Maxwell, formerly Jan Ludwig Hoch, to gain control of this newspaper which I know has your respect, loyalty, and affection—a newspaper as British as roast beef and yorkshire pudding."

The battle dragged on into the new year, with Maxwell's bid now raised to £34 million. Murdoch's victory was finally confirmed after a stormy *News of the World* shareholders' meeting held on 2nd January, 1969, during which Maxwell was repeatedly interrupted by hissing, booing, and loud cat-calls. For him the defeat was a bitter and expensive blow. Afterwards, he said of Murdoch: "He has caught a big fish with a very small hook."

As the result of a complicated deal, control of the News of the World Organisation—valued at that time at £25 million—passed into the hands of Rupert Murdoch's company, News Ltd. of Australia.

After the formalities were over, Murdoch took a house in London with his second wife, Anna, a tall beautiful blonde of twenty-five whom he had met whilst she was a reporter on one of his papers, and their baby daughter. The house, in Sussex Square, had previously belonged to the son of Jack Cotton, the millionaire property tycoon. No one who knew Murdoch's reputation in Australia—where the school of journalism is traditionally much tougher than in Britain—expected him to play second fiddle to the Carr family for long. Although officially only joint managing director of the *News of the World,* he effectively acted as his own editor, working a twelve-hour Saturday, striding around the office in his shirt-sleeves and involving himself in every part of the paper. "It was like coming out of a vicarage tea party into an Australian bar-room brawl," explained one reporter. "Murdoch even tried changing headlines, but he didn't really understand the old *News of the World* formula. We almost had a secret code with our readers. Where we would have put INCIDENT IN A WATER-CRESS BED, he would come along and change it to something like NINE MONTHS FOR SAVAGE RAPE." In June 1969 Sir William Carr

bowed to the inevitable and handed over the chairmanship of
the News of the World Organisation to Rupert Murdoch. Carr
was given the nominal title of president, but had little more to
do with the running of the paper. This still left the editor,
Stafford Somerfield, a flamboyant and doggedly independent
figure. Throughout the year he was to have an almost continual running battle with his new proprietor.

Things nearly came to a head over the decision to print
Christine Keeler's memoirs for the second time. This earned
the *News of the World* an official rebuke from the Press Council and involved Murdoch in a number of attempts to justify
the decision, the most embarrassing of which came during an
edition of David Frost's London Weekend television show on
3rd October, 1969. Murdoch came under heavy fire, and eventually left the studio in a rage. At the time, it was not realised
that the programme was to have tragic significance for the
future of Muriel McKay. For during it there was discussion,
not only of the literary output of Miss Keeler, but also of the
large amounts of money involved in the *News of the World*
take-over. It was made clear that Murdoch was many times a
millionaire and there was mention too of his young wife, Anna.
Later, in trial testimony, it was said that all this had made a
strong impression on two men watching the talk on their farm
in the wilds of Hertfordshire.

Undeterred by such minor setbacks, Murdoch, his keen commercial sense combined with his driving ambition, had turned
his thoughts towards acquiring a daily paper to keep his
presses in Bouverie Street fully occupied during the week. This
was a gloomy time for Fleet Street, with a number of national
newspapers facing an uncertain future because of falling cir-
culations and dwindling revenue. Any saviour, whatever his
methods, was more than welcome.

The paper that was nearest its deathbed was the newest, the
Sun, a broadsheet which as the traditionally left-wing *Daily
Herald* had been inherited by IPC when it took over Odhams
Press. IPC, under the direction of Cecil King, had attempted
to re-vamp the *Herald* by changing its name and launching it
as the *Sun* in 1964, via one of the most spectacular publicity
campaigns the country has ever seen. But the new paper
turned out to be disappointingly similar to its predecessor and

readers continued to desert it. The fight to take it over was to see another scrap between Murdoch and Maxwell, with Murdoch again emerging as the victor. Maxwell wanted to turn the *Sun* into a Labour Party daily, but could not come to a satisfactory agreement with the printing unions. He finally withdrew his offer to buy it on 3rd September, 1969. This left the way open to Murdoch. Because the *Sun* was such a financial embarrassment to IPC, he was able to secure himself a knockdown bargain when he took it over later in the month. But even at the ridiculously low price he paid of £250,000, there were many sceptics in and around Fleet Street who thought he was throwing his money away.

Turning a deaf ear to them, Murdoch set about finding himself a new editor. He chose Larry Lamb, a man very much in his own mould—tough, aggressive, and a prodigiously hard worker. Lamb was then northern editor of the *Daily Mail* in Manchester. Young and good looking, with a wife and three children, he immediately moved south at Murdoch's request. Together, the two men re-modelled the *Sun,* and the paper was launched on Monday, 17th November, as a brash, campaigning tabloid with a healthy predilection for printing pictures of semi-naked girls. On its first morning, the paper splashed the exclusive confessions of a well-known trainer who admitted to doping his horses. The "confessions" continued through the week. Aggressive, earthy, and possessed of a keen eye for a bare breast, the *Sun* represented a new formula for daily journalism, and one which immediately attracted readers. Within a few hours the paper was sold out.

The paper also attracted its critics. These were countered by Lamb: "If we use a nude picture, it is because it is the best picture around that day for that particular slot in the paper," he said. "We seek to inform people. The series we have run, like the "Sensuous Woman and the Love Machine" are quite harmless. There is nothing there that I wouldn't want my children to read. I believe one of the big troubles for a lot of people these days is in sexual relations—not understanding them properly and creating frustration. We aim to take away this frustration by informing and educating the public."

Even before the launch, wind of the impending changes had

reached the ears of Murdoch's competitors, none of whom were happy at the prospect of losing even a single reader. Especially vulnerable were the two other tabloids, the *Daily Mirror*, owned by IPC, and the less successful *Daily Sketch*, owned by the rival Associated Newspapers. From the start, there was little doubt that Murdoch would not hesitate to bite the hand that had fed him: his main target was to be IPC and the five million daily buyers of the *Mirror*. With Fleet Street facing a battle of the tabloids, and the popular papers pulling out every stop they could find, Murdoch desperately needed to reinforce his managerial team at the *News of the World*. He was also aware that in spite of its editorial appeal, the new *Sun* was still sorely in need of advertising.

The man he chose to be his number two and to take charge of the job of winning new advertisers was Alick McKay—his old friend and countryman, and his father's former trusted employee. This did not exactly endear McKay to his former co-directors at IPC, where the cold draught from the *Sun* was just beginning to be felt. "A lot of people were furious when they heard the news," explained one senior IPC executive. As he had previously indicated to the board, Alick McKay quit his post at IPC on 2nd October, 1969, because of failing health. He took with him a generous "golden handshake," reported to be in the region of £40,000. At that time, many of his colleagues were expecting him to return to Australia with his wife. Instead they received a sharp shock. McKay became one of the first of many top IPC men to be tempted down to Bouverie Street by Rupert Murdoch. In December it was officially announced that he had been appointed to the board of the *News of the World*—effectively as Rupert Murdoch's right-hand man.

Murdoch now felt that things were running smoothly enough at the *News of the World* and the *Sun* to enable him to take a much-needed six week Christmas break in Australia. Before leaving, he asked Alick McKay to stand in for him while he was away—although no official announcement was made. Murdoch also offered to lend McKay the company's distinctive blue Rolls Royce (registration number ULO 18F). It was an offer which McKay accepted gladly, without really thinking; the car was obviously more befitting to his new role than his own Austin Princess.

On 19th December, the day that Murdoch was due to leave the country, the whole *News of the World* board held a rare, and sumptuous, luncheon party in a private room at the Ritz Hotel. The menu, which included caviar and chateau-bottled wines, was specially chosen by Alick McKay, whose taste in these things was rather more sophisticated than that of his new chairman. The meal was a jovial one, and even Somerfield and Murdoch, who sat next to each other, managed to forget their long-running feud. After the brandy and cigars, everyone went downstairs to see Murdoch off and wish him bon voyage. One of those who shook his hand and most warmly was the new, temporary chairman of the *News of the World*, Alick McKay.

After Murdoch had driven off to the airport, Somerfield and McKay decided to go back to the hotel and have a few more drinks. McKay was in a cheerful mood. He was looking forward to his spell in charge of the Organisation.

The next day, Alick adopted a routine more suited to his new position. Every morning from now on the chauffeur would pick him up at 9:30 A.M. promptly. He would then drive in the Rolls to the office and in the evening it would call and bring him home again. At the time, it seemed a pleasant enough change. But it was not one that he was to be permitted to enjoy for very long.

Rooks Farm, Stocking Pelham presents a start contrast to the suburban cosiness of Wimbledon. Although situated only forty miles outside London, it lies in a bleak, deserted countryside which gives little indication that the metropolis is nearby. The village, one of three Pelhams in the district, is hardly more than a straggle of houses which runs unevenly along the borders between the counties of Essex and Hertfordshire. Its population of 170 consists mostly of businessmen, retired country gentlemen, and farmworkers. Apart from one small pub, the Cock Inn, there are few local amenities worth mentioning.

Rooks Farm stands apart from the village, isolated at the

end of a narrow, winding, tree-lined lane. Built in the seventeenth century, it is now in a sadly dilapidated state. The cream paint is peeling off the walls and much of the surrounding ten acres of land is overgrown.

In the autumn of 1967, Rooks Farm was sold by a local estate agent, George Tidey, to an immigrant tailor from Trinidad, Arthur Hosein, and his German-born wife, Else. The price originally asked was £16,000, but Hosein knew how to drive a hard bargain. Eventually he bought the freehold for £14,000. Of this, £5,000 was paid immediately as a deposit and the rest borrowed on a mortgage from the Halifax Building Society. The sale was not a smooth one, and Tidey recalls one occasion when Hosein telephoned his house and swore at his young daughter. "She was in tears. When I took the phone, he threatened me. He said he was going to get me. When I said that he had agreed to a delay in taking possession, he said he had not put anything into writing." Furious and slightly alarmed, Mr. Tidey phoned the nearest police station, which was at Bishop's Stortford, eight miles away. "I told the police that I did not take the threat very seriously, but that I thought I should warn them just in case."

Two years after this, the Hoseins were joined at the farm by Arthur's youngest brother, Nizam, who was given a room, weekly pocket-money, and cigarettes in exchange for his services as a labourer. Also living there were the couple's young son and daughter, Rudeen and Fareeda, and Arthur's teenage sister Haffiza, who had recently arrived from Trinidad. Together they formed a bizarre community which was strangely out of place among the predominantly Anglo-Saxon and Tory squirearchy of the surrounding district.

For Arthur Hosein, acquiring Rooks Farm was an important step towards fulfilling a fantasy which had dominated his life since he first arrived in Britain as a prospective student in September 1955. At repeated intervals after that, he told his family, his friends, and almost anyone who could be persuaded to listen that his ambition in life was to become "a country gentleman and a millionaire." In part, this passion was furthered by the feeling, later to be shared by his brother, that he was the victim of the inherent colour prejudice of the English middle and upper classes. But perhaps another motive can be found in the circumstances of his childhood, which was spent among the sugar cane fields of Trinidad.

The Hosein brothers were both born in a wooden, four-room shack in Railway Road, Dow Village. The village was part of the misleadingly named California district of Trinidad, lying just south of Port-of-Spain. Arthur was the second eldest son and was born on 18th August, 1936. His brother Nizam was the youngest son in a family of seven and was born on 1st July, 1948. Their father, Shaffie Hosein, was a strict parent who earned a reasonable living as a skilled tailor, and in his spare time was a respected member of the local council. Both he and his wife, Mrs. Siffiran Hosein, were devout Muslims and they brought up all their children strictly according to the teachings of Islam. Hosein senior was an official of the small mosque in Dow Village, and a framed certificate in Koranic reading took pride of place on the blue and white living-room wall of the Hoseins' house. Despite—or because of—the oppressive religious atmosphere of their early years, neither Arthur nor Nizam displayed any inclination to inherit the beliefs of their parents.

As a child, Arthur showed early initiative and a quick ability to learn. His wit made him popular among his schoolmates. After he left school at fourteen, his father taught him the rudiments of the tailoring business. Four years later, with his parents' blessing, he decided to leave the restricted horizons of Trinidad and seek his fortune in Britain.

Nizam had been a much more difficult child than Arthur. The youngest son in a large family, he had experienced an unhappy childhood. His early feelings of inferiority were reinforced when, after leaving school, he found that he was expected to act as chauffeur to his father. This made him a laughing stock among his young friends. His growing feelings of inferiority and neglect had violent results. On 3rd January, 1968, when he was still only twenty years old, Nizam was convicted of maliciously wounding his father. The case was heard at a Port-of-Spain magistrate's court, and he was lucky to be let off with a warning. Only a few months later, he attempted in a fit of frustration to stab his eldest brother Charles with a kitchen knife, and found himself up before the magistrate once again. On this occasion he was put on probation and bound over to keep the peace on a £33 bond.

By this time, his brother Arthur had already decided to make Britain his permanent home. When he landed in September 1955, his intention had been to become a student. But he soon met problems finding somewhere to study. Running short of ready cash, he settled instead for a job as a £7 a week ledger-clerk in Birmingham.

Arthur discovered, having arrived in this Britain as a young man of eighteen, that he was still eligible for national service. As it turned out, his career in the British army was to be a brief and ignoble one. Even in his late teens, Hosein had acquired a reputation as a boaster and as a man with Walter Mitty-type ideas about his chances of making a material success out of life. While he was still working in Birmingham, he received his call-up papers and became Number 23623918 Private Hosein in the Royal Pioneer Corps. Although he had hardly a penny to his name, his boundless ambition earned him the nickname "Mr. Success" among his mates in the barrack room. He soon found that army discipline and pudding-basin haircuts were not to his taste. He was repeatedy absent without leave, and in 1960 he was court-martialled for desertion. Giving evidence at the court-martial, which was held in Wrexham, one officer said: "He was immeasurably the worst soldier it has been my misfortune to have under me . . . that is, when he wasn't absent or in detention." With the army establishment so determined to quash his dreams of military glory, Arthur stood little chance of acquittal. He was found guilty and sentenced to six months detention in the military prison at Aldershot. Summing up, the Court said: "A very stupid offence, but there is no sign of violence in his character." As Arthur was led away to the cells, he shouted to the assembled officers: "Watch how you go with me. I'll be worth a million one day." He found life hard in the glasshouse. The experience strengthened his growing suspicions of colour prejudice and left him with a lasting feeling of injustice.

After such an ignominious discharge, it was quite in character that he should always boast afterwards of his successful career as a soldier; usually in his stories, 23623918 Private Hosein had risen to the rank of NCO. Very few people were ever permitted to know the real story of one of Britain's most disastrous national servicemen. One of the few was his wife, Else Fischer, whom he met while still in the army, stationed at Colchester Barracks. Although always attractive to women, Hosein had had few lasting relationships. Else was eight years his senior, a tough but good-looking Germanic blonde who had previously had an unsuccessful marriage to a British soldier. When her divorce came through, they were able to get married. For Arthur, this was a new role and he found security in Else, who represented something of a mother-figure to him. She was a level-headed, independent businesswoman who ran her own ladies' hairdressing salon in Mare Street, Hackney. After being discharged from the army, Arthur joined her in the East End and settled down to make a career out of the only craft he really knew well—tailoring. Away from the influences of his brothers, Arthur showed himself a hard worker and a highly skilled trouser maker. He moved into cramped premises above Else's salon in Hackney, and soon found that business was flowing in.

In 1965, Else, by now a mother, gave up her business and became a full-time housewife. On the profits that Arthur was making from his business, the couple moved into a comfortable, semi-detached house at Ongar in Essex. By now, Arthur had sold his business in Hackney and taken the lease on a backroom workshop in Kingsland High Street, Dalston. His skill and speed at trouser-making had earned him respect among the tailoring community in London's East End. One London tailor described him as "the best trouser maker I have ever worked with." Mr. Gerald Gordon, a fellow Hackney tailor, said: "He worked very well and was a very good craftsman." With Britain's boutique boom now in full swing, Arthur Hosein was able to earn up to £150 a week. But his *folies de grandeur* showed little sign of ebbing, and the cockneys with whom he worked dubbed him as "nutty Arthur." Standing about five feet four inches tall, with a neat black moustache, a streak of male vanity, and a tailor's love for snazzy suits, he cut a dapper figure. Had it not been for his unabated urge for a niche among the landed gentry, he might have stayed in the

East End with his wife and family and established a prosperous tailoring business.

But his heart was set on a "country estate." Late in 1967, after making the initial moves to purchase Rooks Farm, Arthur paid his first, and only, visit back to his home in Trinidad. During the time he had been away, he had regularly sent sums of money back to his parents. As his business grew, these had risen as high as £65 a month. On arriving once again in Dow Village, where things had changed little since he had left twelve years before, Arthur began expanding on the fantasies of English life which had already been outlined in his letters. He told his parents and friends that he had a "business in town" and was soon moving to an "estate in the country." But he went a little too far in his elaboration, and seriously upset his father when he remarked that he was going to make money out of pig farming: something that went right against the grain of Muslim belief. To appease his parents, Arthur made a rash promise that he would pay for both of them to fly over and visit him on the farm. However false the picture he painted to this life in England, it was a great temptation to those at home who had never seen beyond the shores of Trinidad. One person immediately influenced was Arthur's younger brother, Nizam, who—as we have seen—was not at all happy in his home environment. In the euphoria of the reunion, sketchy plans were made for him to come over to London to study accountancy.

Before leaving Trinidad, Arthur ran into trouble with the Government, who claimed (falsely) that he was using a forged passport. As a result he was forbidden to leave the country for several weeks and was left kicking his heels. During this time, his business in Hackney suffered badly and he lost much goodwill because of outstanding orders which were left uncompleted; but eventually Arthur succeeded in suing the authorities and was given freedom to leave and compensation of £170.

Once back in England, the Hoseins left their small house in Ongar and moved to the unfamiliar surroundings of Rooks Farm, with its four bedrooms and ten acres of land. Almost immediately, Arthur began what was to prove a long and concerted campaign to ingratiate himself with local society. To boost his standing, he also bought on hire purchase a dark blue Volvo saloon (registration number XGO 994G) to go with the Morris Minor he already owned.

When he arrived at Rooks Farm, Arthur set about furnishing it in a style which fitted in with his preconception of the requirements of a "gentleman's retreat." A large gilt and cream semi-circular cocktail bar was installed in the spacious lounge. Its shelves were well stocked with drink and around it were placed three high stools in matching gilt. The large bathroom was done out in wood-panelling with a matching coral wash basin, bath, and W.C. As soon as the credit could be found, Arthur also set about installing all the expensive domestic appliances that he could afford.

At the back of the farmhouse, across a small, paved courtyard, were a number of outbuildings. They included three piggeries, a barn, and some sheds equipped with two old, fearsome-looking meat tables. Arthur was never a farmer at heart, but he played the part by purchasing some calves, pigs, and chickens. His initial enthusiasm for animal husbandry soon faded and his wife took over most of the unpleasant chores. In one of the sheds, Hosein set up a tailoring workshop. There he would cut trousers, which were then taken to the East End to be finished. He had ideas of turning this workshop into a clothing factory, and once even approached the local council with his plans.

As well as calves and pigs, the Hoseins also kept a pair of savage Alsatians. They were called Rex and Reggie, friendly enough sounding names which gave no indication of the dogs' ferocity. When not in the house, they were kept, chained up, in one of the outhouses. The extent of their viciousness— which became almost a by-word in the village of Stocking Pelham—can be judged from the warning note added by the auctioneers when the contents of Rooks Farm were sold: "It is essential that appointments be made to view as there are two Alsatian guard dogs at the property and applicants are strongly advised not to view without a prior appointment having been made through the auctioneers, so that the guard dogs can be shut up. The auctioneers and the vendor wish to make it quite clear that they can accept no responsibility should applicants fail to observe the above viewing arrangements."

To the villagers Arthur soon became known as "King Hosein." The district was one of those rural backwaters where everyone very soon finds out about everyone else's business. In the bars of the surrounding pubs, Hosein wasted very little time in letting it be known what his business was: to be accepted as part of local society. A heavy drinker, he would invariably order a large whisky with dry ginger ale. He liked to order rounds for other customers at the bar, especially when he could pay in his favourite currency, a ten pound note. On one occasion he let it be known casually that he had £750,000 in the bank, and on another that the Indian High Commissioner had been coming to stay for the weekend, but had been forced to cancel the visit at the last minute. His father was always referred to as an "influential holy man." One man who knew Hosein well was Fred Butler, landlord of the Raven, a small, convivial pub situated at Berden, a village about two miles away from Rooks Farm. "He was forever talking about money and money-making schemes. It was always his boast that one day he would make a million."

Hosein's feeling that he was being discriminated against because of his colour had been increased by some unpleasant experiences with his neighbours at Ongar. It was in no way lessened by his move to Hertfordshire. One incident which tends to bear out his concern happened at the Cock Inn. This tiny pub, about four hundred yards from Rooks Farm, has now changed hands. But one night in 1969, Arthur was asked across the bar if he would like a drink. Hosein replied that he would have a Scotch, and as he ordered, according to one local, "He stuck out his chest as if to say he had at last been accepted." The customer went on, "As the drink was passed to Hosein, three people spat in it. Not because Hosein was coloured, but because he was such an arrogant bastard." Arthur stormed out of the pub in fury, and never returned.

Whether he had been coloured or not, he would still have stuck out like a sore thumb in Stocking Pelham and the surrounding neighbourhood. It is not an area which takes kindly to strangers. Bumptious, garrulous, sometimes loud-mouthed, sometimes entertaining and always an extrovert, he immediately stood apart from the stolid, rural gentry who made up his drinking companions. The strange thing was, he so desperately wanted to become one of them. His ambition for money can be seen as a stepping-stone in this direction; he thought his problems would be solved if he could only buy himself a commission into the gentry. Not all of his Trinidadian background had been forgotten, and often after a few large drinks in one of the local pubs, he would entertain the customers with his own brand of calypso. His favourite butt for criticism was Harold Wilson and the Labour Government, a subject which always went down well among the High Tory majority of the village. Arthur himself claimed to be a staunch Liberal when it came to supporting a political party, but often let it be known in a loud voice that he could personally run the country better than the three main parties put together.

In May 1969, Nizam Hosein arrived in Britain with a six months' visitor's permit, which was later extended to run until January 1970. He had a return charter ticket to Trinidad in his pocket, and very little else. Only twenty-one years old, in both looks and temperament he was quite the opposite of his elder brother. Tall, slightly gangling, with oriental eyes, Nizam was a sullen introvert with none of the bumptiousness of Arthur Hosein. His upbringing had left him with a grudge against society. On the surface this showed itself in a cringing attitude to his elder brothers, of whom he always appeared to be frightened. Underneath was a growing resentment which—as his two court appearances in Trinidad had demonstrated—could spark into violence at the slightest provocation. As it turned out, Nizam would often accompany Arthur on his drinking bouts and on his journeys by car to the East End. In the village he was soon noticed because of his habit of walking the Alsatians dressed in a black leather jacket and a blue steel helmet. "He looked very sinister," explained one housewife. "When I asked him what he was doing, all he would say was that he worked for a Trinidad security company."

The arrival of Nizam brought a change in the atmosphere at Rooks Farm, forcing Arthur to think of more practical methods of fulfilling his twin fantasies of becoming a millionaire and a country gentleman. Nizam was quick to point out the reality of life at Rooks Farm and to compare it unfavourably with the high-flown stories which Arthur had told when he was back in Dow Village. He also reminded him of the invitation which had been issued to the Hosein parents to come and join him "on the estate."

On the night of 3rd October, the two brothers were watching television when suddenly they found themselves faced with an answer to all their problems: the affluence of Rupert Murdoch. They were sitting in the lounge at Rooks Farm when Murdoch was announced as the star guest on the David Frost programme. His main reason for being there was to discuss the controversial Christine Keeler memoirs. But during the course of the programme there were repeated references to his money and to the many millions of pounds which had been involved in his recent takeover of the *News of the World*. References were also made to his pretty wife, Anna. Most people watching were more concerned in the heated argument which broke out between Murdoch and Frost over the memoirs. But at Rooks Farm, the Hosein brothers had other things on their mind—it was almost as if they could see pound notes tumbling down the chimney. Whether the initial plan was evolved in Arthur's galloping imagination or as the result of prompting from the desperate Nizam—who had only a few months of his visitor's permit to run—we shall never know. But from that night it had obviously taken root in both men's minds.

Soon after this followed an undignified row between Arthur Hosein and Captain Charles Barclay, Master of the Puckeridge Hounds and squire of the neighbouring village of Brent Pelham. With his local reputation, Barclay was the kind of man who must have represented the high point of Hosein's social ambition. The two had met on one previous occasion. Late one night, Arthur arrived uninvited on Barclay's doorstep. "I am a wealthy neighbour of yours. I think we should make each other's acquaintance," he said by way of explanation. Rather reluctantly, because it was very late, Barclay invited him inside. Formality was his watchword, and even his teenage children still addressed him as "Captain." But within minutes of settling in a chair, Arthur was referring to him as "Charlie." "Call me Arthur," he said jovially; "I don't mind at all."

On 5th November, 1969, the two men were to confront each

other again. It was a meeting which was to bring Arthur his first, rather fleeting, contact with Scotland Yard. Rooks Farm lay directly in the path of the Puckeridge Hunt, and on the day in question the hounds ran across the corner of Hosein's land, scattering a crowd of chickens. Arthur and Nizam chased them off, brandishing shot-guns. Then Arthur rang the local police to complain of trespassers.

"I met the police on the way up there and explained it was probably me," said Captain Barclay. "The police went to the farm, but did not do anything. So Hosein apparently rang up Scotland Yard, who referred him back to the local police. I was accused of killing chickens and calves—which was quite impossible. I went back to the farm that evening to apologise. I was a bit nervous, as the dogs were extremely savage. After a sticky start, we got on very well. We repaired to the Black Horse (a well-known local pub) and drank quite a lot of whisky. He brought along his wife and brother. But then, the next thing we had was a solicitors' letter which rather surprised us, and which I countered with another solicitors' letter."

Captain Barclay then wrote a personal letter to Arthur and as a result Hosein paid a further visit to his house and the two men drank "a great deal" more whisky together. Arthur was most impressed with the hospitality. Afterwards he wrote a letter addressed to "The Squire" of Brent Pelham. "Dear Charles . . . I must express my worthy thanks to you for your sincerity . . . I am convinced after all you are a gentleman." The incident and the renewed acquaintance with Captain Barclay had further increased Arthur's social ambitions. Soon after, he made a formal application to join the Puckeridge Hunt (although he couldn't ride a horse). Barclay agreed to "consider" it.

The memory of Rupert Murdoch and his millions must have still been haunting Arthur. On 13th December he was given the opportunity he wanted to further his plans. That day his wife, their two children, and his thirteen-year-old sister, Haffiza, left Rooks Farm temporarily. They were making a Christmas visit to Else's parents in Germany, and were not due back in England until January 3rd. Once they were left alone at the farm, Arthur and Nizam began to plot the details.

The first problem they had to solve was the whereabouts of the Murdochs' house; if they were going to kidnap his wife, they would have to do it from her home. Finding the answer was more difficult than they had ever imagined. Having found nothing in the telephone directory, or via directory enquiries, they made a journey to the local library to look in Kelly's Street Directory. But this was no help, so it was decided to drive down to the *News of the World* headquarters in Bouverie Street. It was there that the brothers spotted the blue Rolls Royce. This gave them another plan for tracing the address. It was in keeping with Arthur's enormous conceit that he was contemplating carrying off the first-ever kidnapping in Britain without enlisting any help from known criminals. He did not even contemplate asking for advice from the underworld.

Meanwhile, unaware of the existence of the hamlet of Stocking Pelham, Rupert Murdoch and his wife Anna flew back to Australia on 19th December, 1969, leaving Alick McKay temporarily in charge at the *News of the World*.

On the same day, Nizam Hosein borrowed his brother's Volvo and drove from Rooks Farm to the Greater London Council's offices at Country Hall in Westminster.

Showing little of his usual reticence, he approached one of the girl clerks in the vehicle registration department. He said that he had been involved in a minor accident a few days before, and was trying to trace the owner of the other car. Nizam gave his name and address as Mr. Sharif Mustapha of Norbury, London. He made out a formal application form, using an address which much later was traced back to one of his cousins. The girl took little notice of the enquiry at the time: it seemed genuine enough. She checked the files for the name of the owner of a Rolls Royce, registration number ULO 18F, and discovered that it belonged to the News of the World Organisation of Bouverie Street. To Nizam's obvious disappointment, she was unable to provide him with any more information about the home address of the owner.

Nizam drove anxiously back to Rooks Farm and told his brother of the failure of the mission. Now they had to resort to less reliable means of trying to discover the vital piece of information. Behaving like the amateur criminals they were, they decided that there was only one alternative left open to them: to lie in wait near the *News of the World* office and follow the Rolls Royce home. This they did, completely failing to notice any facial differences between the man who climbed into the back seat and Rupert Murdoch, whom they had watched so intently on television only two months before.

At this time, Muriel McKay was busy preparing to leave St. Mary House for Christmas, which the couple were planning to spend with their daughter in Lingfield, Sussex. It was to be a festive season that was to end in the most appalling way.

At Rooks Farm, the Christmas period was marked with jitteriness and ill-feeling between the two brothers. Even with their plan so near to fruition, they found time to row over Nizam's girl friend, a pretty Trinidadian nurse of twenty-seven, Liley Mohammed. Arthur had first introduced Nizam to the girl, whose sister he had known in Trinidad. On Boxing Day, having finished hospital duty, Liley made her way to Rooks Farm. Soon after, the two brothers began to fight viciously over her and Nizam was beaten up. He was so upset that he left the farm briefly and telephoned a complaint to the local police about Arthur's behaviour. Later he returned, to find the terrified Liley still there. In the morning she left, promising to get in touch with him again soon. Three days later, Liley telephoned Nizam to make another date. She phoned first at 8:00 P.M., but there was no reply from Rooks Farm. An hour later she phoned again, but there was still no response.

It was the evening of Monday, 29th December. Both Hoseins were out of the house. Only Muriel McKay had the misfortune to know their business.

2
DISAPPEARANCE

ON MONDAY, 29th DECEMBER, 1969, Britain was just beginning to pick up the threads after the long Christmas break. It was a bitterly cold morning with a heavy frost. At their home in Arthur Road, Wimbledon, Alick and Muriel McKay awoke early. They still had a little unpacking to do, having returned only the previous day from Lingfield in Sussex, where they had spent a relaxing Christmas with Diane and David Dyer. Over breakfast, they discussed the prospect of getting back to their familiar routines: Alick to Fleet Street and his wife at home. As they had no specific engagements for the evening, they planned to spend it together in front of the television.

At 9:30 A.M. punctually, the dark blue Rolls Royce lent by the absent Rupert Murdoch pulled into the drive, ready to take Alick to the *News of the World* offices. Muriel had a brief word with Bill, the chauffeur, and then waved her husband goodbye. The parting was affectionate, casual and, entirely normal—the same as it had been throughout the eleven years the couple had lived at Arthur Road.

A few minutes later, Mrs. McKay put on a warm coat and went to the garage to get her own car, a Ford Capri. It being Monday, she had to drive to Haydon's Road on the other side of Wimbledon to pick up the family's regular household help, the elderly Mrs. Marjorie Nightingale. The drive took about ten minutes, and after comparing Christmas experiences the two women returned together to Arthur Road. For the rest of the morning, Muriel McKay busied herself around the house. Knowing that she had to go to London in the afternoon to visit the dentist, she prepared an evening meal. She decided on steak, and took two large fillets out of the fridge, leaving them garnished and ready to cook on a plate beside the grill. At midday, Mrs. McKay walked up to Wimbledon Village to do some shopping. She took an old pair of shoes to the cobbler's to be dyed and then went to her local bank, where she cashed a cheque for £25. After that, she went along to her favourite dress shop, Anne Forshaw. The shop is a small, fashionable, and expensive boutique situated only a few hundred yards up from St. Mary House. Mrs. McKay was a popular customer and knew the staff well. She was in a cheerful mood that morning, and spent thirty minutes choosing an outfit. She decided on a pretty matching silk dress and evening coat which suited her well. It cost £60, and as she was not planning to wear it straight away, she told the shop assistant that she would leave it and pick it up later.

Her shopping finished, Mrs. McKay wandered back home and ate a light lunch in the kitchen with Marjorie Nightingale. The two had known each other for a number of years. They sat and chatted until it was time for Mrs. McKay to keep her dentist's appointment. Mrs. Nightingale stayed behind at the house to finish her work. After that she would settle down to watch television until her employer returned. At the dentist's, Mrs. McKay had a routine check-up. She arrived back at St. Mary House at five o'clock, took off her expensive town coat and left it over a chair in the kitchen, planning to hang it up later. She put a reversible black and brown car coat over the simple green jersey suit she was wearing, got the car out again and drove Mrs. Nightingale home. On the way, she stopped briefly to buy copies of two London papers, the *Evening News* and the *Evening Standard*.

At 5:30 P.M., still without an apparent care in the world, she left Mrs. Nightingale at her home. Mrs. McKay drove straight back to St. Mary House, and arrived there ten minutes later. She was a woman who enjoyed her role as a housewife and felt few of the frustrations that can often result from an over-domesticated existence. It had been pleasant to get back to the routine of her home after the Christmas holiday, and now she was going to settle down in front of the blazing log fire and wait for Alick. Having reached Arthur Road, Mrs. McKay put her car in the garage beside her husband's Austin Princess. She then locked the door and went into the house to make a cup of tea.

The ground floor of St. Mary House is spaciously laid out. The entrance is through a large outer door which leads by way of a small porch to an inner door. Three months previously, the McKays had been burgled, and this had made Muriel very nervous at the thought of intruders. Since then, she had insisted firmly that the chain should be kept on the outer door at all times. The inner door opens on to a large hallway and lounge. Straight ahead is the staircase and beyond, on the left, the dining-room and kitchen. The house is furnished in an expensive but unostentatious style. On the wooden floors are Persian rugs and in the rooms the decor is typical of many an upper middle-class English home. Muriel had insisted on one folksy touch, and the mantelpieces, desks and table-tops were covered with a series of framed family portraits.

When Mrs. McKay got home, she made the tea and then went through the large lounge to the cosy "snug" which opened off it at the rear. This was the room used by the couple when they were alone. It was small and homely, heated by an open log fire-place, with a television, a telephone, and a couple of deep armchairs. On the walls were some of Mrs. McKay's own still-life paintings, and on this particular Monday, the occasional Christmas decoration. With Mrs. McKay was her adored pet dachshund, Carl, who was curled up sleeping peacefully at her feet. At about 5:40 P.M., she turned on the television, but, as was her habit, kept the sound off until it was news time. Then she settled into one of the armchairs to read the evening papers.

What happened then, nobody knows for certain—and it is unlikely that anyone ever will. All we can do is judge from the evidence that was left behind and from the testimony of the only neighbour who passed the house during the fatal two hours before Alick McKay returned to find it deserted. That was Mrs. Mona Lydiatt, who lived close by at number 43 Arthur Road. At exactly 6:00 P.M., she walked past the front of St. Mary House. A casual glance through the gate told her that the light outside the front door was on, as were the lights in the other downstairs rooms. She also saw a "dark coloured car" parked in the drive Without giving it a second thought she continued on her way home.

Quite oblivious that anything was wrong, Alick McKay arrived back at Arthur Road at his normal time of 7:45 P.M. After a long and tiring day at the office, he was looking forward to a good dinner and a relaxing evening with his wife. Having dismissed the chauffeur and the Rolls for the night, he stopped momentarily to pick up a page of the *People* newspaper which was blowing about in the drive. He thought nothing of it at the time, crumpled the paper up and tossed it into a nearby flower bed. Then he went to the front door and gave three short rings on the bell followed by one longer one. This code had been worked out after the burglary in September and was designed to prevent Muriel from opening the door to strangers at night. Getting no reply, Alick thought his wife might be dozing and rang again. Still no one answered, and he tried the door. To his amazement he found that it was unlocked and that the chain was off, hanging down in its unused position.

As soon as he opened the inner door into the hall, Alick realised that something was seriously wrong. His wife's shoes were placed neatly where she had left them on the bottom step and her shopping basket was on a chair. But at the bottom of the staircase, her black leather handbag was lying open, with its contents strewn up the first five steps. The white telephone was lying upside down on the floor, with its lead pulled out of the wall, and the number disc on the dial was missing. On a table in the hallway was an opened tin of Elastoplast sticking plaster, on a nearby chair an untidy bale of thick twine, and beside that, lying on the desk, was a rusty-looking meat-cleaver or bill-hook with a wooden handle. On the floor, by the fallen telephone, Alick found his wife's reading spectacles.

Fearing that there might still be an intruder in the house, Alick McKay grabbed the meat-cleaver off the desk and rushed up the stairs brandishing it and shouting his wife's name. There was nothing but an ominous silence. He came down the stairs again and began searching frantically through all the rooms on the ground floor. What he had already seen immediately indicated that something sinister had taken place in the house. This sense of disaster was increased by what little evidence he could find of his wife's fate.

First he went into the "snug," the small room at the back of the lounge where Muriel usually sat when she was waiting for him to come home. There he found the television turned on, an evening newspaper open by his wife's chair, the dachshund Carl sitting on the floor, and the log fire still burning. What immediately caught his eye was the disturbing fact that the fire was not guarded. Some months before there had been an accident with one of their dogs. Ever since, Muriel had been extra careful to protect the fire if ever Carl was to be left on his own in the house.

Next he went into the kitchen. There he found the expensive coat Muriel had worn on her travels that day still lying over the back of a chair. He also found the supper that she had prepared that morning. Two steaks were lying on a plate beside the grill, prepared and ready to cook, indicating again that if Mrs. McKay had left of her own accord, she had gone off in a great hurry. By now, Alick was utterly confused: had his wife run away? If so, why and with whom? Had she been forcibly abducted? If so, why had she been taken? If not, then just where the hell was she? Alick's suspicions that she had been taken against her will were strengthened when he discovered that some jewellery and some cash was missing from his wife's open handbag. The jewellery included an emerald and platinum eternity ring set with diamonds, a gold and pearl pendant, three bracelets, and an emerald brooch. Later a value of about £600 was to be put on the missing items.

His next step was to call the police. This he did from a neighbour's house, having first enquired whether they had seen or heard anything that might give an indication of what had happened; but no one he spoke to could add anything to the little he already knew. Alick telephoned Wimbledon Police Station at exactly eight o'clock. Ten minutes later, the first policeman arrived at St. Mary House, quite uncertain what to expect. He was a small, uniformed inspector, a Scot called Anderson, who had answered a call from the station over his patrol car radio. Although missing women cases are customarily dealt with by the uniformed police, there were a number of factors which immediately made Anderson feel that this was a job for the C.I.D. (Criminal Investigation Department). After a brief inspection of the house, he telephoned the station to request reinforcements.

Throughout the McKay Case, there has been much confusion

over telephones: early on, people jumped to the false conclusion that some or all of the phones at the house were out of order. In fact all were working except the one in the hall which had been pulled away from the wall. But even this was not broken; once the lead was pushed back in the socket it worked perfectly again.

The senior C.I.D. man on duty at Wimbledon that night was Detective Sergeant Graham Birch. He had already heard whispers about the disappearance and immediately made his way up to the house when he was requested by Anderson. From the beginning, the police were well aware of both the national and local implications of the case. The police are always wary when dealing with people of great wealth, and around Wimbledon they had more than their fair share of these. Only recently Birch had handled a burglary at the house of the local M.P., Sir Cyril Black. With regard to Alick McKay, they knew at once of his influential Fleet Street connections, and of his recent controversial move from IPC to the *News of the World*. This was to have a marked effect on their handling of the case.

Birch arrived at the house to be met at the door by McKay. He was immediately and forcibly struck by the man's apparent calm. Birch was puzzled: he could not believe that someone who had just lost his wife would act in this self-controlled, phlegmatic way. McKay took Birch inside and showed him the empty handbag, the rusty meat-cleaver, and the upturned telephone. He also indicated that the lock on the inner door looked as though it had been forced. His first words were "My wife has gone. What has happened? Where has she gone?" Birch was instinctively put on his guard by the situation he found inside St. Mary House: something unusual had certainly happened, but it seemed very much as though the chaos had been purposefully created. While Alick McKay could see only the changes, Birch could see only the order. "The scene looked very much as if it had been set up for an amateur production of an Agatha Christie thriller," Birch explained later. "The keys and other oddments from the handbag dribbled down the stairs like a neat row of confetti." Birch's reaction—to be supported later by more senior detectives—was that the scene had been set deliberately, probably by Mrs. McKay herself. As one

Scotland Yard official commented, "We have many cases of women in their early fifties 'disappearing'—and sometimes they do like to make their exit in a theatrical manner."

Birch went back with Alick to the dining-room, and over a glass of whisky they had a long talk about the family and its background, concentrating on Alick's relationship with his wife. For a detective, Birch is a sensitive, sympathetic man. As tactfully as possible, he suggested that Mrs. McKay might have left of her own choice, pointing out that this was a fairly common occurrence among middle-aged housewives. But McKay was visibly hurt at the suggestion, and was insistent that this was not the case. "No," he said firmly, "I know my wife better than that." From the start, Alick had to live with the innuendo that his life with Muriel had not been all that it appeared on the surface: it was a suggestion that the police had to investigate if they were to do their duty, and which the press quickly picked up. As with many other early suggestions in the case, it was completely untrue—yet the man who knew the truth, Alick McKay, was not being entirely believed. In desperation McKay was searching through memories of his own recent behaviour to see if there was any part of it that might have given Muriel the urge to run away; but he could think of nothing.

Birch was in a dilemma, because here was a case where a number of immediate explanations would fit the circumstances —and yet none of them stood out clearly enough to be obvious. What was missing, among the numerous possibilities that could explain the disappearance was any indication of a motive. Because of the missing jewellery, robbery sprang instantly to mind. Perhaps she had disturbed a burglar who wanted to prevent her calling the police? But Birch's feeling that the house was just too tidy for this was later shared by his superiors. Also the only items missing had come out of Mrs. McKay's handbag; there was no sign that any other of the many valuables in the house had been touched. The immediate conclusion drawn by detective sergeant Birch was that Mrs. McKay had left St. Mary House for personal reasons. But, was it another man? Was she ill? *Or* had she simply run away as the outcome of some bitter family argument?

As soon as Birch discovered that the McKays had two married daughters living in the home counties, he was anxious that they should be rung in case they had heard any news. But, reluctant to cause unnecessary worry to his children while there was still hope, Alick hesitated to make the calls. This put the police even more on their guard. Later on, detectives were to say of the McKay case that on the first night "the whole thing smelt."

By a cruel irony, Alick McKay, the newspaper tycoon, had found himself in just the kind of situation where he was creating his own news. At that moment he needed a friend, someone in whom he could confide. He also realised that his wife's disappearance was soon likely to become a major story. The obvious choice seemed to be to ring Larry Lamb, editor of the *Sun*. The early edition of the paper had already gone to press, but Lamb was still in the building supervising the late news schedule. He knew McKay from his IPC days and decided to drive straight down to Wimbledon to see if there was anything he could do to help. Aware that he was dealing with what was potentially an explosive story, Lamb, who had a reputation as a hard newsman, alerted a reporter and photographer and told them to go to the house.

Meanwhile at Arthur Road more policemen had begun to arrive. Uniformed officers stood guard both inside and outside the house. Mrs. Nightingale had also returned in a police car, having been questioned to see if she could give any reason for Mrs. McKay's sudden disappearance. The elderly household help could only repeat that Mrs. McKay had seemed perfectly normal during the day and had displayed none of the signs of a woman who was secretly planning a disappearing act. Having said her piece, Mrs. Nightingale retired to the kitchen to get on with the job of preparing tea and sandwiches for the visitors.

Over a glass of whisky, Birch continued to interrogate Alick McKay. Although McKay was not then aware of it, he was himself a prime suspect. "This was very much the same sort of situation as when a woman comes to a police station alleging that she has been raped," Birch explained later. "First you have her medically examined and then interrogate her to try to break her story down." Once more, McKay went through the details of what he had found at the house when he arrived, of his relationship with Muriel, and of his behaviour during the day.

Together McKay and Birch searched the rooms and the attic at St. Mary House. Although they found that a jewellery box appeared to have been disturbed, there was no sign that the rows of expensive clothing in Mrs. McKay's fitted wardrobe had been touched; as far as McKay could see all his wife's possessions, apart from those she had been wearing during the day, were still at the house. In police terms at least, he continued to act with what they regarded as unusual calm.

At Birch's request, Alick McKay then rang Diane Dyer and broke the news, and after that Jennifer Burgess. Both women were shocked and said that they would drive to Wimbledon immediately with their husbands.

By now, the *Sun* reporter had arrived at Arthur Road, and the police on the spot were faced with the question of what they were to tell the newspapers. The reporter was anxious for guidance about what he could file to his office: after all, it was a story that intimately concerned his paper's top management. A *Sun* photographer had also come to the door, but was forbidden by Birch to enter the house. As a life-long newspaperman, McKay's instinct was to favour publicity. He knew that in the past newspaper stories about missing people had proved one of the best ways of recovering them. He was also aware of the popularity and success of the *News of the World's* own Missing Persons' Bureau. Birch on the other hand felt strongly that neither the police nor the family interest would be served by newspaper speculation. Eventually a compromise was reached. Lamb gave his reporter a short statement and told him to dictate it over to the *Sun's* night news desk. He also gave instructions that the statement was to be passed on to the Press Association, the national agency which provides all British papers, television, and radio services with home news stories. "I also gave instructions to our night news desk that they were not to use any information or give any detail that was not available to the Press Association," Lamb explained later. "I was very anxious that we should not seem to be taking advantage of the situation."

Once the story went out over the Press Association wires, it had the inevitable repercussions. The phone in the small, cosy sitting room at St. Mary House began to buzz with calls from questioning reporters. Most of them were answered anonymously by Lamb, who said tersely that there was nothing more to be added to the statement. The first press inquiry to Scotland Yard was made just after 10:00 P.M. by a journalist from the *Sun*. He wanted to know if there was any fresh information about Mrs. McKay and was told there was not. The Yard then alerted Andrew Henderson, the District Liaison Officer (DLO) for the South Western district, which includes Wimbledon. Henderson, who would be in charge of official press relations in the area, was at home, and was told only to take further action if other papers began to ask questions.

Having gone as far as he could with his initial questioning, Birch decided that it was time to ring his two superior officers, Detective Chief Superintendent Wilfred ("Bill") Smith and Detective Inspector John Minors. In his own mind, he had no clear idea of what had happened to Mrs. McKay, but felt that, for one reason or another, she had probably left the house of her own volition. Smith had only recently been appointed head of the C.I.D. division which covers Wimbledon. When Birch rang, he was at home and listened while the details of Mrs. McKay's disappearance were explained to him. Birch also rang Minors, but he was out. He was given instructions by Smith to handle the whole affair with caution.

If one is surprised by the reticence being shown by the police in these early stages, it has to be remembered that each local division of the force deals in terms not of one "missing woman" case a week but of five or six. Here, there was a further restraining factor. The new *Sun* was less than two months old, and already its shock tactics had raised a number of disapproving eyebrows; within less than two hours of Mrs. McKay's disappearance, the paper—including its editor—was much in evidence at Arthur Road. It was an understandable, if totally incorrect, assumption by the police that they might have become involved in an elaborate publicity stunt.

Approaching midnight, the number inside St. Mary House had been swollen by the arrival of more police and relatives. The atmosphere was tense. But McKay, at least, was sitting quietly, inviting the police to help themselves to his drink and cigarettes. Underneath his calm exterior he was beginning to become irritated, feeling that the detectives were not taking things seriously enough. Perhaps he also sensed that they had reservations about his own account of his wife's character and recent behaviour. In the circumstances, this kind of reaction was to be expected from a man who suddenly, without reason, finds that he has lost his wife. It was to be markedly increased by the arrival of Diane Dyer and her husband, David. An attractive young woman with dark hair, Diane had inherited Mrs. McKay's looks and was very close to her mother. She was deeply upset by what had happened. David Dyer was a tough businessman whose experience and temperament were not fitted to playing a passive role. He felt that immediate action was ncessary, and to lift the strain from his father-in-law, he took charge of the situation in the house. This was to bring him into sharp conflict with the police.

Soon after Dyer's arrival at St. Mary House, an enterprising reporter from the *Daily Express* rang Stafford Somerfield, editor of the *News of the World*, to ask whether he could shed any light on the mystery. Somerfield, who had been at home all day, knew nothing about Mrs. McKay's disappearance. He had been a friend of the family for a number of years, and immediately rang Arthur Road to find out what had happened. Alick spoke to him, and after telling him the full story, confided that he was not at all happy with the attitude of the police. He told Somerfield that they were not being very helpful and that they seemed to doubt that his wife had been taken away by force. As the long-time and hospitable editor of the largest selling newspaper in Britain, Somerfield had close connections with a number of the top men at Scotland Yard. Also, knowing the couple well, he immediately shared Alick's conviction that something tragic had happened to Muriel McKay: "She was a woman who was interested in good works and the church, and she was passionately fond of her home and her children," he explains. "I know she was just not the type to run away." In an effort to relieve Alick's sense of frustration, Somerfield rang John DuRose, the Deputy Assistant Commissioner in charge of all operational departments at Scotland Yard: when it comes to pulling strings in the police, one could not have gone much nearer the top. DuRose was in bed when the call came through, and replied that he had never heard of Mrs.

McKay, let alone of her disappearance. Somerfield reminded the Deputy Assistant Commissioner of Alick McKay's importance in Fleet Street. He pointed out that the unexplained disappearance of his wife would very soon become a front page story.

The implications sank in. After Somerfield had rung off, word very quickly reached Wimbledon. As one policeman there commented, "The wheels were now in motion."

At midnight, when Graham Birch was relieved by another colleague from Wimbledon, Detective Sergeant White, there was still no conclusive evidence to show that Mrs. McKay had been the victim of kidnapping. The attitudes of those inside the house contrasted sharply. On the one side was the family, plus some friends such as Lamb. The visual evidence combined with their knowledge of Muriel's character was quite enough to convince them that she had been taken away by force. What else could explain the bale of twine, the sinister-looking meat-cleaver, the sticking-plaster, and the general state of the house.

On the other side were the police, who as a general rule never like to jump to immediate conclusions about the nature of any crime. The possibility of kidnapping had certainly entered their minds, but there were a number of factors to be set against it. The frequency with which women of Mrs. McKay's age are reported missing put the police very much on their guard. There was the possibility that Muriel had run away with another man, or that her husband was himself somehow implicated. Perhaps most significant was the complete absence of any kind of ransom demand. At this early stage, the amateur's analysis was to prove nearer to the mark. Birch himself was not over-convinced by the meat-cleaver, which McKay claimed to have found lying on the desk in the lounge. "At the time, I felt it was the type of garden tool that might have been found in any suburban garage," he said.

At the beginning of any investigation, the British police tend to work on a percentage basis, weighing up first one possibility and then another. According to Commander Guiver, the chief C.I.D. officer involved, the official view at this time was "95 per cent in favour of her going away of her own choice, and only 5 per cent of her being taken away."

Although it was now into the early hours of Tuesday morning, people were still arriving at St. Mary House. Soon after midnight, the McKays' other daughter, Jennifer, reached Arthur Road with her husband, Ian Burgess. By temperament, he was a much more placid character than David Dyer, and was ready to leave the problem of locating Mrs. McKay in the hands of the police.

Another early morning visitor to the house was Hugh Cudlipp, then chairman of the International Publishing Corporation. Many pressmen were surprised to see him, following the ill-feeling they knew to have resulted from McKay's switch from IPC to the *News of the World*. But as well as being a long-standing former colleague of Alick's, he was also a close friend of the family. Before leaving, Cudlipp had a brief and informal goodnight word with reporters waiting in the cold outside the house. He told them that at that stage the police did not seem to be certain that anything more than a disappearance was involved. If anything, this strengthened the view that Mrs. McKay had left for reasons of her own.

As a result of the Press Association statement, reporters from other daily newspapers, and some local freelances, had begun to arrive at Arthur Road. On orders from McKay and the police, they were not permitted inside the house. Instead they settled down to a long night in cars parked up and down the road. By this time, Andrew Henderson, Scotland Yard's District Liaison Officer had also arrived, having been forced out of bed after learning that the house was "under siege" by pressmen. The top crime specialists of the national dailies had been alerted at home, but most of them shared the early police view that Mrs. McKay had left St. Mary House deliberately. "At that stage" said one, "there was no other workable theory to go on."

The first public announcement of the affair came over the BBC's 1:00 A.M. news bulletin. In a brief item, the newsreader reported that the wife of the "deputy chairman of the *News of the World*" had disappeared in mysterious circumstances from her home. Neither her name nor address was mentioned.

Exactly fifteen minutes later, at 1:15 A.M., the telephone at St. Mary House rang again. By this time, Dyer had assumed control. He answered, thinking it was yet another call from

Fleet Street. Instead, a male operator spoke and said he was putting through a call from a telephone booth at Bell Common, Epping, a town in Essex. Dyer gave his name and was answered by a muffled voice: "Tell Mr. McKay it is M3, the Mafia." Taken aback, Dyer immediately summoned Alick to the phone, which was in the small sitting-room, and indicated to Detective Sergeant White that he should listen on an extension in the kitchen. The conversation then continued:

CALLER: This is Mafia Group 3; we are from America. Mafia M3; we have your wife.
McKAY: You have my wife?
CALLER: You will need a million pounds by Wednesday.
McKAY: What are you talking about? I don't understand.
CALLER: Mafia. Do you understand?
McKAY: Yes, I have heard of them.
CALLER: We have your wife. It will cost you one million pounds.
McKAY: That is ridiculous. I haven't got anything like a million.
CALLER: You had better get it. You have friends. Get it from them. We tried to get Rupert Murdoch's wife. We couldn't get her, so we took yours instead.
McKAY: Rupert Murdoch?
CALLER: You have a million by Wednesday night, or we will kill her. Understand?
McKAY: What do I do?
CALLER: All you have to do is to wait for the contact. That is for the money. You will get instructions. Have the money or you won't have a wife. We will contact you again.

Before the perplexed Alick McKay could say more, or discover any specific instructions for paying the ransom, the receiver at the other end was put down. For a moment he stood transfixed. Then he put back the receiver, turned and described the bizarre conversation to the waiting family and policemen. Among the McKays, the first reaction was a mixture of relief and bewilderment. Any word about Muriel was preferable to the suspense of total silence. But this relief was tinged with horror as they realised that what they had been fearing all along was true—she had been kidnapped.

Here again, the family view was sharply contrasted with that of the police. In spite of their perplexity, the McKays at least believed wholeheartedly that the call was genuine, if only because it was the one straw they had to grasp at. The conversation with the mysterious M3 plunged Alick McKay even deeper into despair: he was being asked to pay an impossible sum of money and given no instructions what to do with it. Cruelest of all, the anonymous voice and the threats summoned up gruesome visions of the kind of treatment being meted out to his wife.

On the police side, there was an instinctive caution which exasperated some members of the family. White's first reaction, once he checked his notes, was to phone his superior, Chief Superintendent Smith. He also took all the details from the Epping operator, who telephoned back to the house after the call was over. The operator himself had actually listened in to the early part of the conversation with M3. In public, the police were not committing themselves to a view about the call: they tried to give the impression of keeping an open mind. But in private, they felt certain it had been a hoax. In addition to the fantastic sum being demanded, there was the fact that the call had been put through the operator rather than made through the automatic STD system. This hardly seemed the kind of naive behaviour to be expected from a gang of ruthless kidnappers, let alone from the Mafia! The police were well aware of the acrimony that had surrounded Alick McKay's departure from IPC. That, combined with the fact that news of Muriel's disappearance had long ago been given out by the Press Association, made them suspect this first ransom call as a vicious hoax from someone inside IPC anxious to get their own back on McKay. If not, it was probably some Fleet Street joker with a sick sense of humour.

Because none of the detectives had seriously entertained the prospect of a telephoned ransom demand, there were no recording facilities available at St. Mary House that morning. For evidence of M3's actual words, all there was to go on was the operator, Alick's memory, and Detective Sergeant White's notebook. Considering that one of the very few hard facts the police possessed from the beginning was that the telephone number disc was missing, it is an indication of their initial scepticism that they had made no effort to install a tape-recorder.

Soon after the call, Lamb made a tactful exit: it was a moment when the family wished to be by themselves. The Burgesses and the Dyers had all volunteered to stay at the house with Alick McKay. They decided to take turns manning the telephone throughout the night. Everyone was hoping for further word from M3, but the instrument was to remain silent. Meanwhile, Smith, who had been awakened in bed with the news of the call from M3, had dressed, and was now on his way round to Arthur Road. Outside the door of St. Mary House, in the icy December morning, two uniformed police officers stood on guard. The mystery had only just begun.

3
KIDNAPPING
OR FAMILY FEUD?

Tuesday, 30th December

MOST OF THE country read about Mrs. McKay's strange disappearance over the breakfast table. As a result of the Press Association statement, the story appeared in all the morning papers, although none carried any mention of the 1:15 A.M. telephone call from M3. Predictably, the *Sun* laid the most emphasis on the affair, splashing the story across its front page under the banner headline "MYSTERY OF PRESS CHIEF'S MISSING WIFE." The paper also printed a smiling photograph of Muriel McKay and played up the angle of the missing jewellery. Above the headline was another strip of bold type: "LONDON HUNT AFTER GEMS RAID."

Among some members of the family and a few of Alick's close friends, Lamb was criticised for his early handling of the case. It certainly played into the hands of those policemen who were still convinced that the whole affair was nothing more than a newspaper stunt. Lamb was in a tricky position, having access to a major story at a time when he was struggling, with only a small staff, to boost the sales of a newly launched newspaper. In playing up the mystery he had an ally in Alick McKay, who was convinced at this stage that publicity was the best approach and the one most likely to secure the return of his wife.

By the morning, though, the shock was beginning to tell on Alick: his face was haggard and pale, and there were grey bags under his eyes. In his stead, David Dyer handled all the family's contacts with the press.

One of the early visitors to the house after breakfast was Lamb, who came to talk with Alick and to see if there were any fresh developments. It was a routine he was to repeat every morning during the early days of the case. Soon his aggressive, journalistic attitude was to upset some members of the family—not all of whom were convinced that maximum publicity was the surest way of getting Muriel back. They felt that the subject should have been less sensationally handled.

Two important factors had now combined to increase the intensity of the police operation: the arrival of the first ransom demand and the informal approach from DuRose at Scotland Yard. During the morning, all three senior members of the police team in charge of the investigation visited St. Mary House, which by then was surrounded by an army of inquisitive reporters and television cameramen. In overall charge was Commander Guiver from Scotland Yard, a sturdy, lantern-jawed individual with many years of police experience behind him. Directly under Guiver were Chief Superintendent Smith and Inspector Minors, both from Wimbledon. Of the two, Smith, with his habit of always sporting a jaunty bow tie, was the more extroverted. An approachable, portly man, his looks contrasted strongly with those of Minors, who fitted the more conventional image of a British detective: tall and burly with broad shoulders, sleeked-down black hair and a pencil-line moustache.

After a hectic night, Smith visited St. Mary House for the second time the next morning. With him was Andrew Henderson, the District Liaison Officer. One of the first things to be decided was how to deal with the ever-increasing numbers of pressmen who had been assigned to cover developments in Wimbledon. After some discussion, Henderson was given permission by Smith to release certain details of the conversation with M3 at a press conference to be held at the police station. Henderson was given permission to mention the million pound demand, but he was told to make no reference at all to the allegation that the intended victim had been Mrs. Rupert Murdoch.

Already the official description of Mrs. McKay had been distributed to neighbouring police forces. Its strict, formal language did little justice to the warm, motherly woman whose life was now hanging in the balance. It described Muriel McKay as "5 ft. 9 in., medium build, dark complexion, dark brown hair, straight nose, green eyes, oval face," and said that she was thought to be wearing a green jersey suit and a bracelet, a wedding ring and two diamond rings.

As in all missing person cases, the next thing that had to be done by the police was the creation of a "crime index." This is a complex and meticulous filing system in which every piece of information, however seemingly petty or irrelevant, is placed and related by an elaborate system of cross refrences. Smith appointed Detective Sergeant Jim Parker to handle the important job of compiling and looking after the index. He was the ideal man for the job, reliable, hard working, and methodical, with an uncanny knack for handling detail. During and after the case he played the unsung hero's role of backroom boy. The importance of the index is emphasised by Commander Guiver: "If you haven't got a good one going within forty-eight hours, you are as good as lost on a complex job like this one. A detective's job is to solve whatever particular crime he is dealing with: above all, he wants to get someone up in that dock. On so many occasions, it is the index which provides the evidence."

The publicity surrounding Mrs. McKay's disappearance had already begun to have its repercussions. By 9:30 A.M., the switchboard at Wimbledon Police Station was jammed with calls. Most of these were from the press, but there was also a steady flow of calls beginning to build up from the public. Some were genuine offers of useful information, others were from cranks—but no matter what the source, every one had to be noted down and methodically filed. The lines were so congested that the police enlisted the help of the Post Office* who sent up a team of engineers to install extra lines. Until they had completed their work, the station was virtually cut off from outside communications, with every existing telephone line blocked by incoming calls.

In a busy police station, it is never easy to find a spare room, but the index and its staff had to be housed somewhere. Eventually it was decided to set it up in a small, cramped room on the first floor which had previously been used by trainee

---

* In Britain, the Post Office is the government department responsible for the telephone system.

detectives. Off at one corner of the room, Smith and Minors were provided with a tiny office of their own. Already the two detectives had issued orders to the men under their command and they were now preparing to embark on a rigorous thirty-six hour session that would leave no time for sleep. Their job was to follow every possible lead in an effort to get some indication about how and why Mrs. McKay, a supposedly innocent and untroubled housewife, had vanished without trace from her fireside. Some policemen began a methodical check of all car owners in the area, some visited the local shops, others interviewed Mrs. McKay's neighbours and friends, and a further group was ordered to look into the recent activities of all known criminals and cranks in the district. Question and answer papers were hastily printed, asking people to state where they had been between 5:30 P.M. and 7:30 P.M. on the previous day.

One of the early visitors to Wimbledon Police Station was Terence Underwood, the late-night telephone operator from Epping. He was closely interrogated by detectives, and he detailed all that he could remember about the call he had put through in the early hours of the morning to 946 2656, the home of Alick McKay. Underwood told police that he had listened in to part of the call and described the man who made it as having "an American or a coloured voice."

Statements running into hundreds were brought back to the station and handed to Parker for filing. Often the significance of clues was not immediately realised. One of these was a report from a local resident. At 4:40 on the afternoon of 29th December he had been driving from Wimbledon towards Putney on the road which runs alongside the common. He overtook a Volvo car and saw men inside talking together. One was of "tanned Arab colour," while the passenger was wearing something over his head. Ten minutes later, the same motorist saw the Volvo again, this time turning into Church Road, which leads towards the McKay house. This piece of information meant nothing at the time: it was also quite impossible to take it any further without checking the ownership of each of the 33,000 Volvos then on the roads in Britain. The time and expense involved did not justify such a step. It was, after all, just one of the dozens of cars which had been reported in the area that day. Only after the Hoseins had been taken into custody did the Volvo sighting take its place in the reconstruction of the events which led up to the kidnap. The statement was discovered buried deep in the main index of witnesses' statements, cross-filed under "Volvo" and broken down again into sightings of "Two Men."

One of the first steps for the detectives was to match Mrs. McKay's disappearance with another case from the same area. Eight months before, Mrs. Dawn Jones, a middle-aged Wimbledon housewife, had also disappeared from her house for no apparent reason. The circumstances were uncannily similar to those at Arthur Road. The electric fire in Mrs. Jones' sitting-room had been left switched on and the contents of her handbag were found scattered on the floor of a bicycle shed behind the house. Weeks later, she was discovered lying dead on the floor of a mountain hut in the Scottish Highlands. She was identified by comparing her fingerprints with those on her belongings at home. Mrs. Jones' house was not far from Arthur Road, and initially the police looked into the possibility of a link between the two crimes. But it was not an idea they took seriously for very long.

Even Guiver, with his long and distinguished record as a detective, admitted to being baffled by Mrs. McKay's disappearance. "It was the most bizarre crime I had ever been faced with. Usually you have a starting point—a body, a weapon or stolen property. Here we had nothing, as the amount of jewellery taken was really insignificant. It just didn't look like a robbery; the place was too tidy."

What the police did have was a record of the one million pound ransom demanded by M3—the so-called Mafia. Although British experience of the Mafia had been mercifully restricted to one or two fringe companies in the London gaming-club business, the police were unable to dismiss the prospect entirely at this early stage. "We had nothing to show us either way," says Guiver. It was noted at Wimbledon that kidnap was a crime in which the Italian Mafiosi were particularly well versed. At this stage, the police were treating the disappearance with an open mind. Although they were still inclined to the idea that Mrs. McKay had walked out, the connection with Fleet Street—and therefore the danger of public criticism—had caused them to employ many more men than would have been asked for in a run-of-the-mill missing person inquiry. Smith and Minors virtually abandoned all the other work in hand and passed it down to their subordinates. With Alick still a prime suspect, a more thorough search of the attic and the gardens at St. Mary House took place. During the morning, it was decided that two detectives would be stationed permanently at the house, working in eight hour shifts. The McKays were hospitable and extremely good cooks, so the job was a popular one among the junior men at Wimbledon. But it was not easy. There was a strong undercurrent of friction between the family and the police, which Smith was trying hard to penetrate.

Twenty hours had now passed since the disappearance was reported and the police still had no real idea how or why Mrs. McKay had gone. On the family side, there was a feeling that police bureaucracy was hindering rather than helping with her recovery. They had all been finger-printed, had given an account of their movements, and seen the house and garden searched repeatedly by teams of policemen. They felt in a way that the police were looking in the wrong place: instead of being around Arthur Road, they should have been out scouring the countryside.

Inside the house, the first priority was the installation of a recording device, in anticipation of another call from M3. As one detective pointed out, "Even if the caller was a crank, he was a dangerous one and we had to try and track him down." In this Britain, the Government and local authorities, who share the costs of the police, supervise their spending very closely. Consequently the police are often unable to obtain equipment that they need, and are short of even the elementary requirements of a modern organisation. Everything from cars to typewriters are in short supply, and tape-recorders are rarely available. For a policeman to get a tape-recorder through the normal channels would take at least a fortnight —and that is only for the necessary documentation. It may take another week for the machine to arrive. The McKay case was to show how necessary it is for a police force to be properly equipped if it is to work efficiently.

To meet the immediate emergency, one of the detectives

working on the investigation offered to fetch his own tape-recorder from home. It was a portable, £30 model—not sophisticated, but adequate for the purpose. The offer was readily accepted and the detective came round to Arthur Road to fit the machine and to explain to his colleagues and the family how it worked. A suction pad was attached to the white telephone receiver in the snug, which the police had now commandeered as their headquarters. There was another extension in the hall, the one that Alick McKay had discovered unplugged the previous evening; this was now working again, and was being used by the family. Whenever one of the duty detectives answered a call, he would always announce himself as one of the McKays. As soon as a tape was used up, it was taken down to Wimbledon police station to be transcribed by a civilian stenographer. The results were then entered in Parker's rapidly expanding index.

By mid-morning, news of the one million pounds ransom call had been carried in the early editions of the evening papers and on the radio bulletins. It had been officially released by Henderson at the morning press conference held at the police station. Information about the call had been doctored to meet the police needs and neither the public nor journalists knew anything about the alleged mix-up over Rupert Murdoch's wife, the code sign M3, or the fact that the kidnappers claimed to be members of the Mafia.

Even so, the new wave of publicity and banner headlines displeased some senior police officers. But it was proving difficult to keep anything quiet in a house where pressmen were entertained as guests and where publicity was regarded as an asset. Outside Arthur Road, a growing huddle of British and foreign journalists were waiting for any snippet of information that came either from the house or from local police contacts. In every profession, not least that of politics, there are always those who, for various reasons, are prepared to talk to the press. And policemen are no exceptions to the general rule.

Before lunch, Alick received another influential visitor, Stafford Somerfield, editor of the *News of the World*. The two were of the same generation, and Somerfield became something of a confidant. He played a major role in finally convincing the police that Mrs. McKay had not disappeared as part of a publicity stunt for the *Sun*. "In my view, they were very stupid ever to regard it as a stunt," he says. "They should have known better." But it is hard to blame the police for at least having suspicions in that direction. The press itself had equally far-fetched, though unpublicised, views about what had happened to Mrs. McKay. Three Fleet Street papers assigned a reporter and a photographer each to keep a round-the-clock watch on the country home of the chief of a fourth national paper. All believed the newspaper bar gossip that Mrs. McKay was involved with another man or was part of a murky vendetta within Fleet Street.

With hardly any sleep in the previous thirty hours, Alick was beginning to show the emotional and physical strain of Muriel's disappearance. Over and over again he was retracing in his mind the scene he had found at the house when he had arrived back the night before. He insisted on showing Somerfield where the inner porch door appeared to have been forced. McKay also showed him a number of the postcards which Mrs. McKay had written to her children whenever she had been away. "Even if she has run away," said Alick, "I know she would never have done it without giving us some indication of where she is." The whole family was experiencing a restlessness brought on by sheer impotence—the inability to do anything constructive about finding Muriel. David Dyer felt this particularly strongly, much more so than Ian Burgess.

The police had contacted McKay's bank manager and cancelled the joint account which the couple had shared. By this time, they were aware that about twenty-five pounds had disappeared from the open handbag, as well as the missing items of jewellery.

The number of phone calls from cranks, both to the police station and to Arthur Road, was already beginning to reach unmanageable proportions. Often for as long as half an hour, the line to St. Mary House would be jammed by a succession of callers. Some would prove to be harmless "breathers," some would shout foul-mouthed abuse, and others would provide false leads. These were the most time-wasting and led to a continuing succession of "theories" about the reasons for Mrs. McKay's disappearance. On this first Tuesday, the family were also disconcerted by the number of press inquiries which were helping to block up their telephone lines. In desperation, they asked all papers to direct their questions to Wimbledon police station.

During the day, David Dyer was particularly impressed by one call from an anonymous woman, who muttered two words —"Grey Hillman"—in a faint voice before the line suddenly went dead: another false lead which the police had to take seriously. It was just one of hundreds which had to be methodically investigated. The plodding thoroughness of much British police work is a constant subject for satire on television and in the press. It is something we almost take for granted, but it often has excellent results. Yet it is easy to appreciate the mounting frustration of Alick McKay and the Dyers at the cautious pace with which the police were working.

By early afternoon, with no more sign from M3, belief in the genuineness of the first call was beginning to fade. The police had started totting up the hundreds of individuals connected with the worlds of press and broadcasting who could have learnt of Mrs. McKay's disappearance before the call was made. The melodramatic guise of "Mafia Group 3" strengthened the suspicion that it must have been a hoax. On the family side, there was a growing sense of desperation: if Muriel had been kidnapped by some sinister gang, why were they being given no indication of how to go about getting her back? Already Alick had received offers from a number of wealthy friends to help make up the million pounds.

At 4:30 P.M. the family were sitting in the lounge discussing some of these points. Two detectives were also there manning the tape-recorder. It was now a full fifteen hours since the call from the Epping phone box. Every time the phone rang in the house, the tension increased; but as the number of cruel hoaxes began to mount, hope was weakening.

At 4:59 P.M. the phone in the lounge rang again and was answered by David Dyer. The first thing he heard were the pips which indicate that a call is coming from a telephone box. Then as watching members of the family saw the sudden change of expression on his face, they realised that he must be talking to M3 for the second time. Again, there was the deep, muffled voice at the other end of the line. "Your wife has just posted a letter to you," it said. "Do co-operate, for heaven's sake. For her sake, don't call the police. You have been followed. Did you get the message? Did you get the money?" With that, and without any further explanation, the phone went dead. Dyer replaced the receiver and recounted the message to the family.

The police had this call on tape and two detectives played it back in the lounge of St. Mary House. It made bizarre listening. An immediate attempt was made to trace it through the operator. But M3 had improved on their technique. This time they had used the automatic STD system which, as the police have discovered to their cost, makes it impossible to trace individual calls.

This second contact from the mysterious M3 put the McKay family very much on tenterhooks. Now they had to endure the suspense of waiting for the promised letter. It was almost as if M3 was deliberately trying to crack their nerve. The call reinforced those inside the police who were beginning to accept that Mrs. McKay actually was the victim of genuine kidnappers; but others were far from convinced.

That night, Diane appeared on the 8:50 P.M. BBC Television News, making an emotional appeal for the safe return of her mother. On the screen she looked upset and worn out by her ordeal, and immediately won the sympathy of viewers. Her television appearance added to the welter of publicity surrounding the case. This was rapidly infuriating the police, who felt that it was seriously interfering with their inquiries. "The one thing we wanted was for the publicity to die down," Guiver commented later. But although the police did not realise it on this first day, the ballyhoo surrounding the case had hardly begun. Because David Dyer had taken charge of the family side, he was to bear the brunt of police criticism. Since he desperately wanted the return of his mother-in-law, it is understandable that he should have been prepared to adopt unconventional methods. But inevitably this prevented his seeing eye-to-eye with the detectives.

That evening, the family settled down to what was to become a depressingly familiar routine. Two detectives were seated in the snug, where they were able to keep a close eye on the tape-recorder. On this occasion they ate a meal cooked by the two daughters; on others, they would bring their own sandwiches. It being so close to Christmas, Alick still had healthy supplies of drink and cigarettes in the house, and he continued to offer them around generously. Throughout the night, the members of the family took turns staying awake and answering the telephone. Some read, others talked about almost anything in an effort to reduce the nervous tension. Recalling M3's warning about not calling in the police, some of the McKays felt unease at the presence of the two strangers sitting in the back room. It was understandable if at times they might have wished to be dealing with the matter on their own.

In and around Wimbledon, thirty policemen and detectives were continuing with their enquiries. Neither Smith nor Minors had slept; it was too early in the investigation for any letting up. The case had even managed to capture the limited imaginations of the top civil servants at the Home Office, which was then in the hands of James Callaghan. Like many members of the public, attracted by the mass of conflicting publicity, the civil servants were naturally curious. They were also interested for more serious and professional reasons. If this really was a kidnapping, it would be Britain's first—and as such would raise some important questions about the general problem of the maintenance of law and order. There was a feeling among both civil servants and senior policemen that there was an additional, compelling reason to catch the offenders. Criminals, like children, are born imitators, and if this first kidnap was to succeed, who was to say where things might stop? A realisation of this attitude at the top must have had repercussions, however unconscious, lower down the ranks. Although the police might have thought that the prime motive was the safe recovery of Mrs. McKay, in their minds it was proving impossible to distinguish that from bringing to justice the man, or men, who had seized her.

Wednesday, 31st December: New Year's Eve

In addition to the hundreds of telephone calls, both St. Mary House and Wimbledon police station were now being inundated with letters about various aspects of the case.

On Wednesday, one among the many brought the first communication from Mrs. McKay. Indirectly it was to further the tension which had already built up between the family and the police. Postmarked "6:45 P.M., 30.12.69, Tottenham N. 17," the envelope, addressed to Alick McKay, arrived at St. Mary House with the morning post. Inside was a piece of lined blue writing paper, and across it in a faltering, almost illegible hand was a pathetic plea from Muriel McKay: the only words that had been heard from her since she disappeared. Alick read the letter in company with Larry Lamb, who was paying his customary morning call to the house. McKay immediately recognised his wife's handwriting.

From its appearance, it was obvious that the letter had been written under duress. The sentences were clipped and the words cramped and misaligned: "Please do something to get me home. I am blindfolded and cold. Please co-operate for I cannot keep going. I think of you constantly and the family and friends." It concluded with the plea of an innocent and bewildered woman: "What have I done to deserve this treatment?... Love Muriel."

The letter left Alick with mixed feelings. By now, he personally needed no convincing that Muriel was being held against her will; but the letter, which had been promised in the second phone call, was further evidence that she really had been kidnapped by a gang calling itself "M3." It was encouraging to have some sign that Muriel was alive, but not in this form. The letter implied that his wife was being mistreated and that she was in desperate straits. There was also no indication about how he could help her. Alick was still as much in the dark as ever.

The contents of the letter and details of the postmark were telephoned to Chief Superintendent Smith at Wimbledon police station. After some discussion, it was agreed that they should be kept secret and not revealed to any pressmen. Because he felt that Mrs. McKay's remarks were highly personal, Smith ordered his men not to make any mention of them to journalists. His word was obeyed, and nothing was said about the letter at the official press conference. These conferences had now been introduced on a regular basis and were held at Wimbledon police station twice daily, at midday and 6:00 P.M.

Nevertheless, the contents of the letter did appear in full in most of the papers the next morning. This was to cause great annoyance to the police and to do much to exacerbate the ill-feeling between them and the McKay family. Even today, there is a continuing dispute about how the words of that all-important first ransom letter found their way to Fleet Street.

The first that Smith heard of the leak was early on Wednesday evening while he was having a drink in a local Wimbledon pub with Andrew Henderson, the DLO. The two men were approached by a senior reporter from the *Sun* who told them that he knew about the letter and warned that his paper was going to print it in full the next day. This infuriated Smith, who felt that it was a sign of a complete lack of co-operation on the part of the family. Anxious to find out the truth, he drove straight to Arthur Road and confronted Alick McKay. Smith spoke severely to all the family, and reminded them of the firm agreement which had been made that morning: no mention of the letter was to be made to the press. Alick then rang Lamb at his office and confirmed that details about the letter were going to be published in the *Sun*. But Smith was determined that all the papers should be treated equally. He therefore rang the Press Association and dictated to them the letter's contents.

This incident was more bitter than the other clashes between the police and the family because Smith and his colleagues felt that their position was being seriously undermined. They were also hurt because the decision not to release details of the letter had been taken in good faith to protect the family's feelings. The police felt that the contents were highly personal and should be kept private.

Larry Lamb has a different view about how the letter became public: "The McKay family didn't release it. The contents of the letter were released by the police." Lamb says that after agreeing with Alick McKay and the police at St. Mary House not to mention it, he heard nothing until late in the evening when he received an urgent message from his night editor. The call from the office asked for his guidance: "The P.A.," it said, "are running a story about the letter." Lamb's orders were that the *Sun* should print everything that came over the Press Association tapes, and nothing more. Later he put his side of the case. "The police intimated that I had released the contents of the letter because the *Sun* had it first. The simple answer is that we publish earlier than the other Fleet Street dailies and the police saw the *Sun* first." Printing only in London, the *Sun* has to come off the presses earlier than its rivals in order to fly copies to Scotland and Northern Ireland.

Commander Guiver, on the other hand, is insistent that the letter was released to the press "by the McKay family and their associates." The senior detectives involved in the case felt that the continual flow of sensational publicity was making their job impossible. Every fresh revelation was bringing in its wake a mass of false information which was rapidly clogging up the detection machine.

In the circumstances, a clash of opinions was inevitable: many members of the family just could not agree that publicity was against their best interests, if—as they honestly believed—it might help to bring Muriel back. Dyer, especially, was coming round to the view that the McKays should be permitted to make their own deal with the kidnappers, even if it meant the police making a temporary withdrawal. This was a method which had proved successful in a number of famous kidnapping cases abroad. Perhaps Alick's attitude did not go so far as his son-in-law's: he certainly never suggested openly that the family should go it alone. But he still had a disturbing conviction that the police were not doing all that they could. For that reason, his support was lent to any of the efforts by the younger members of the family to step up the search.

That night Smith and the McKays discussed what the next steps should be. The superintendent felt it necessary to take the family into his confidence. This was very unusual, because the police traditionally work in great secrecy and rarely tell the complainant anything at all. Here, because of the extraordinary circumstances, the police were almost forced to work as closely as possible with the family. One move that was agreed upon was that Diane should again be allowed to appear on television, this time on the ITV network, where she was to make a further emotional appeal for the kidnappers to make some kind of contact. Also, both daughters and David Dyer made the short journey to Wimbledon police station to attend a press conference organised by Smith. For all his dislike of the publicity, he felt it was imperative to go along with the family to some degree if he was to establish an understanding with them; for that reason he invited the younger McKays to attend the conference. But Alick was deliberately kept in the background.

In answer to a question at the conference, David Dyer said that a letter had been received from Mrs. McKay. He added, "We are completely certain that she is held captive somewhere, but there is nothing definite about any ransom." Later, on their return to St. Mary House, Dyer summoned the reporters who were waiting outside. They huddled round him as he read out a further statement.

"Mr. McKay has received no difinite instructions as to how he is to pay the ransom money. On behalf of Mr. McKay, I wish to pass this message to the person or persons concerned: 'Will you please inform me what I have to do to get my wife back? What do you want from me? I am willing to do anything in reason to get my wife back. Please give me your instructions and what guarantee I have that she will be safely returned to me. I have had so many cranks communicate with me that I must be sure that I am dealing with the right person.' "

Dyer also told the waiting pressmen that the family were encouraged to hear from Mrs. McKay, but were worried and puzzled at the lack of definite information.

He was acting as front-man partly on his own initiative and partly on advice from the police. Smith wanted the press to give the impression that Alick's condition was much worse than it really was, hoping that this might encourage the kidnappers to make some more positive moves. The police also wanted an excuse to prevent his answering the phone at St. Mary House because they felt he was too emotionally involved, and thus inclined to do too much of the talking. What they wanted was someone who would draw M3 out, and perhaps tempt them to give some clue to their identity or whereabouts. In reality, although McKay was naturally suffering from shock, depression, and exhaustion, his physical state was not nearly as bad as the stories implied. He had certainly not suffered another heart attack.

After Dyer's appearance on the steps of St. Mary House, there was another call which was to lead to a further worsening of the conflict between the family and the police. It was from a nurse, who told Dyer that she was "praying" for all the McKays and that she could put them in touch with a good medium, who might be able to discover the whereabouts of Mrs. McKay. She gave them the name and address of a member of the Spiritualists' Association, which has its headquarters tucked away incongruously among the foreign embassies in Belgrave Square. Although it was now into the early hours of New Year's Day, the telephone at Arthur Road was still ringing periodically. In this unhappy atmosphere, the New Year was seen in with little enthusiasm and no champagne. All present were hoping against hope that it would soon bring some indication of the whereabouts of Muriel McKay.

It was decided that David Dyer should contact the medium in the morning. The use of mediums was something which had not until then occurred to the family. Dyer explained the family's view later when a sceptical reporter asked how much faith they put in spiritualists: "We are living on crumbs because we have had no facts since the letter." This was the basic difference between the family and the police. The McKays were a close-knit group and they were all emotionally involved. Much as they may have tried, they were quite unable to sit back quietly and take a detached attitude: they were people used to giving orders and making decisions. The police, on the contrary, did not want to be seen getting worked up about nothing. It was over forty-eight hours since Mrs. McKay had last been heard of, and they still had no definite idea what had happened to her, although they were now inclined to the view that it was a kidnapping. Their objectives were to keep publicity to a minimum and to continue with their enquiries. They were acutely conscious of the professional ridicule they would have to face if spiritualists were seen to enter the case.

Thursday, 1st January: New Year's Day

If Fleet Street is ever short of facts, it can always be relied upon to be long on speculation. The group of journalists involved full-time with the case had by now evolved three separate theories to explain Mrs. McKay's disappearance, all of which had just enough substance to make them credible. The most popular theory argued that Mrs. McKay had staged her own exit from St. Mary House and made her way back to Australia. It was said that she had been made unhappy when Alick chose not to return there. But what the pressmen did not know was that provision for a regular lengthy visit to Australia was written into McKay's contract with the *News of the World*. It was also suggested that Muriel might have been the victim of a band of Australian gangsters. It was widely known that in the 1960s Australians had begun to infiltrate London's underworld. They were noted among both criminals and the police for their toughness. Among the rackets which they had organised successfully were a series of armed bank raids and shopliftings on a military scale.

A further idea, taken seriously at the time, was that Mrs. McKay had been seized by a group of militant Zionists. This arose from a belief that she might have been mistaken for Mrs. Margaret McKay, the then Labour Member of Parliament known for her pro-Arab sympathies. Mrs. McKay sat for a constituency which bordered on Wimbledon and was known to have incurred hostility among Israeli sympathisers in Britain.

There was a fourth suggestion: that she had run away with another man. But even the most sensational British papers have some sense of decorum, particularly when it comes to dealing with one of their own, and this was not a theory that was publicly floated with much enthusiasm.

In addition to these theories about the causes of Mrs. McKay's disappearance, there was also another put forward to explain why she might already have died of natural causes. This relied on the knowledge that Mrs. McKay was taking a regular dose of cortizone for her arthritis. It was argued that the shock of a sudden cut in supplies might have killed her. In fact, the size of her daily dose was so small that the idea was not treated at all seriously by those who were in the know.

Although refusing to debate any of these suggestions in public, the police were doing their own speculating in private. Initially, they paid some attention to the possibility of Mrs. McKay's wanting to return to Australia. A number of detectives thought that the first ransom letter might have been a blind to put them off the trail.

News of Muriel's disappearance had already been broken to her son Ian by reporters in Australia, and he was now on the way to England with his wife Lesley. His arrival at Wimbledon was to be the turning point in the fragile partnership existing between the McKay clan and the police.

Another central character who had been told in Australia was Rupert Murdoch. His shock on hearing the news was even more pronounced: as well as being a close friend of the McKay family he was also informed in the strictest confidence that the intended victim of Mafia Group 3 had been his own wife, Anna Murdoch offered to come straight back to London. But he was strongly advised to stay put in Australia by the British police. They were not prepared to take any risks. If the kidnappers really did exist, the police were afraid that on hearing of Murdoch's return they might make a second kidnap attempt. Badly shaken by the news, Murdoch remained on his guard and did not return to England until February.

In his continued absence, Alick remained acting chairman of the *News of the World*. Every morning, the blue Rolls Royce would pull into the drive at St. Mary House carrying the important papers which he still had to deal with. Although under immense personal pressure, he had to go through the motions of meeting his new business responsibilities.

During the morning, Dyer rang the telephone number that had been given to him by the anonymous nurse. It was a sign of the family's desperation that they were already turning to spiritualists for help. The spiritualist said that she would not be able to meet the family to "meditate" because she was already booked up until the following month. But she did offer some crumbs of encouragement, claiming to have already received a "message" about Mrs. McKay which indicated that three people had been involved in her abduction and also hinted strongly at an unspecified address in the Seven Sisters Road. This impressed the family, as part of the road ran through the London postal district where the first ransom letter had been franked on the Tuesday evening.

The spiritualist also told them that Muriel had been moved once since leaving Arthur Road and was now being kept in what she described as "a very scruffy place." The motive for the abduction was spite or malice, said the medium. She could see no reason at all for money coming into it. This new idea, that Mrs. McKay's disappearance might be the result of spite, or more specifically part of a vendetta against the *News of the World,* was to gain validity during the day.

Spurred on by the spiritualist's insights, the family decided to try to enlist the help of the most famous clairvoyant in the world, Gerard Croiset. Perhaps better known in his native Holland, or across the Atlantic in the United States, Croiset had been involved with British crimes in the past. One of the most spectacular was the Moors Murder Case, where he helped those trying to find the hidden graves of the murdered school children. Once a grocer's clerk, Croiset at the age of sixty resembles an eccentric professor. He has piercing blue eyes, a shock of bushy grey hair and a penchant for loud check suits. By 1969 he had already been exercising his undeniable powers for some forty years, and was known to be responsible for discovering, among other things, the whereabouts of more than 500 missing school children. In most languages, Croiset would be described as a clairvoyant, but in Holland, where since 1946 he has been attached to the well-known and respected Parapsychology Institute at the University of Utrecht, he is called a paragnost. This is a word coined by his mentor, Professor W. C. H. Tenhaeff, from the Greek words *para,* meaning "beyond," and *gnosis* meaning "knowledge."

It was quite in keeping with the strangeness of Mrs. McKay's disappearance that on New Year's Day, 1970, attention should shift from Arthur Road to a small house on a tree-lined street in the Dutch town of Utrecht. It was here that Gerard Croiset had his home, dividing his time between spiritual healing, parapsychological experiments, and solving missing person cases from all over the world. He prefers to work at home, as this lessens the chances of misleading images coming between him and his subject. Anyone disposed, as are some British policemen, to dismiss his work as complete mumbo-jumbo would be well advised to take some time off to study the records of his achievemer ts, which are meticulously preserved at the Institute. These include tape-recordings, stenographic transcripts, and accompanying statements confirming their accuracy from the police and eyewitnesses. Croiset's assistance has been officially requested by the Dutch police on a number of major crimes.

In the case of Mrs. McKay, the Dutchman was first approached via a telephone call from Eric Cutler, a senior British advertising executive and a close friend to Alick. Having talked to the clairvoyant briefly, Cutler took a plane to Holland. With him he carried only a framed photograph of Muriel McKay and a map of London and the suburbs. This initial approach by telephone was necessary, because Croiset—who never charges a fee for his services—will put his powers to use only in cases where his social conscience is aroused. He will have nothing to do with predicting the results of lotteries or horse races. "Don't come to me to ask about burglaries, break-ins, stolen bullion, or diamond robberies," he says, "because I am just not interested in anything to do with money."

When Cutler's plane took off, the police were still unaware that the family had decided to engage the help of the Dutch medium. Had the McKays not allowed the fact to leak out to the press, the detectives might never have become so annoyed.

Having arrived in Utrecht, Cutler made straight for 21 Willem De Zwijgerstraat, the modest house where Croiset lives with his blind, grey-haired wife, Gerda. He handed the clairvoyant the photograph of Mrs. McKay and waited for some response. For Croiset, a photo, personal jewellery, or clothing acts rather like an aerial when he is trying to locate someone who is missing: his mind works exactly as if it were a television set with the sound turned off. He sees a succession of picture images, which he often scribbles down in rough, childlike drawings to try to make clearer what appears in his mind. To watching outsiders, it is an uncanny process.

"The impression I get is of a white farm," he told Cutler. "Around it are trees and a green barn." The conversation took place through a Dutch interpreter, as Croiset, despite his wide international experience, speaks only a few words of English. The clairvoyant then went on to describe details of another, nearby farm, which he explained would provide a guiding point to one where Mrs. McKay was actually being held. He pointed out certain distinctive landmarks which he saw, including a deserted airstrip, a concrete building, and an old motor-cycle, half submerged in a shallow pond. Croiset stressed ominously that he was quite certain that Mrs. McKay had been taken against her will. "If she is not found within fourteen days, she will be dead" he warned.

Surprisingly open about his second sight and its occasional fallibility, Croiset will always indicate if he is in any way uncertain about the impressions which he receives. On this occasion he was adamant that he had correctly located the immediate surroundings of the missing woman. What was much more difficult was to try to determine the exact geographical location of the farm he had seen, a problem exaggerated by his scant knowledge of the English countryside. Croiset had once visited St. Paul's Cathedral and used it as a convenient starting point to try to re-trace, through images, the journey made by Mrs. McKay's kidnappers on the fatal night. Their route, he claimed, had taken them on a road heading north-north-east out of London (the use of nautical language is common among paraphyschologists). He then proceeded to map out the road and its direction.

Like many of the people who meet Croiset face to face, Cutler was impressed by his obvious sincerity and his manner of working. The Dutch clairvoyant uses none of the ploys of the spiritualist: he never enters a trance or seeks to summon the help of supernatural powers. He shows signs of extreme concentration, and combines them; when his interest and conscience are aroused; with a very human desire to help. "Sometimes," he admits, "the ordinary human feelings get the better of my powers as a paragnost. I want too much to discover somebody's whereabouts and this seems to prevent me receiving the correct impressions." In time, this blurring of his two personalities was going to effect Croiset's handling of the search for Mrs. McKay.

Having gleaned this early information, Cutler immediately telephoned the McKay household in Wimbledon. Although by no means conclusive, the information gave them new hope; and whether or not one believes in the powers of extra-sensory perception, Croiset's advice did lead the police searchers to a deserted building on the Essex-Hertfordshire border. But they found nothing; and the details of the incident were dutifully filed away among the many different lines of enquiry then being pursued. It was only much later that it was revealed how close Croiset had come to pointing his finger at Stocking Pelham and Rooks Farm. He maintains to this day that the searchers only went as far as the first farm he had indicated. "That was only meant as a guideline. My impressions told me that she was being held in another one a few miles away."

The recourse to mediums illustrated once again the split that had formed between the police and the McKay family: in the view of many closely involved with the case, it did more to widen the gap than anything else. This was not only because of the British policeman's natural—almost inborn—distrust of such unconventional methods. If it pleased the McKays to put their trust in clairvoyants, the detectives did not object—in a way, it was a help. It kept the family occupied, when otherwise they might have been under an intolerable emotional strain. And if they could find some outlet for their energies, it meant they would be less trouble to the police.

What really annoyed Commander Guiver and his men was the McKays' insistence on publicising the fact that a leading spiritualist had been consulted, especially someone with the international repute and news value of Gerard Croiset, who instantly became the subject of feature articles and imitation by his lesser known English and Continental equivalents. Guiver describes Scotland Yard's reaction: "Because of Croiset's intervention, we wasted thousands of man hours. Not through following up his ideas, but because of all the imitators."

The McKay case and the stimulus provided by the association with Gerard Croiset started a new wave of telephone calls and letters to St. Mary House and to the overworked staff at Wimbledon Police Station. Within a few days, this was to have serious consequences, although few of the amateur mediums can have realised the extent of the trouble they were causing: because of the colossal public response to the case, M3, it was later discovered, was finding it almost impossible to transmit his demands to the waiting family.

That afternoon, though, there were to be just two more calls from him before a silence that lasted for nine days. Frustratingly for the police, the calls were once again made on STD from an untraceable number. At St. Mary House, the phone was answered by Diane Dyer. After some opening remarks, explaining who she was, the call continued:

M3 : I want to speak to your daddy.
DD : Well, he's not in very good health, I'm afraid.
M3 : Well, where's your mummy; can I speak to her?
DD : I'm sorry I don't know where my mother is . . . Do you have any idea?
M3 : I'll contact you later.
DD : Well, why don't we talk now? I mean, I'm here. I might not be here later.
M3 : You've gone too far; it has gone too far now.
DD : What's gone too far. There's nothing gone too far, you know . . .

Without giving her a chance to continue, M3 put down the receiver, leaving Diane in mid-sentence. But before anyone had much time to speculate on what was meant by the grim warning of matters having "gone too far," the telephone rang again. It was M3 on the line once more. This time he was more specific:

M3 : They've got to get a million, a million pounds. I'll contact them tomorrow and they have got to get it in fivers and tenners.
DD : Where do you get a million pounds from? I wouldn't know.
M3 : Well, I don't know. That's not my business.
DD : Well, if you want it, it is your business, isn't it?

At that, M3 rang off for the second time, leaving the family still in suspense. Although they felt certain that these calls were coming from genuine kidnappers, there was still no indication at all about how any business deal was to be reached. Also, amidst the continuing flow of calls from hoaxers of all ages and sexes, it was almost impossible, without the advantage of hindsight, to pinpoint the real criminals.

This factor was emphasised at the evening press conference, held in the dingy surroundings of Wimbledon police station.

Journalists were asked to inform their readers that work had been hampered during the investigation by "numerous calls to the house which are obviously the work of cranks. Several times the phone has rung, Mr. McKay has picked it up and there has been nothing but heavy breathing at the other end." But even this direct appeal to the public for their co-operation had little effect. The flow of calls continued to mount. By the end of the week, the police calculated that more enquiries had been received and dealt with than during the first month following the Great Train Robbery.

Why did the public identify itself so closely with the plight of Mrs. McKay? Publicity had generated a degree of outside interest that the British police had never experienced before. Also, for the ordinary man and woman in the street, there was a genuine sympathy for the despair of Alick McKay and his family. As no motive had been discovered, there were still many millions of people who were able to think, "There but for the grace of God. . . ."

Alick McKay's close connections with Fleet Street were to dog the whole investigation. Another motive examined both in the press and by the police arose from the fear that Mrs. McKay had been seized as the innocent tool in a vendetta against either the *News of the World* or one of Murdoch's Australian papers. It was even being mooted that she had been kidnapped as an act of revenge against the *News of the World* for one of its past exposés, or as a hostage against a story currently being pursued by the paper. Perhaps a probe into the Mafia's influence in Britain?

The *News of the World* had only recently come in for widespread criticism for its decision to pay many thousands of pounds for the chance to print the memoirs of Christine Keeler for the second time. When Cardinal Heenan, leader of the Roman Catholic Church in Britain, announced he was going to withdraw an article in protest, Stafford Somerfield cheekily asked why he was turning down the opportunity to preach "to sixteen million sinners on a Sunday."

The theory that Mrs. McKay had been kidnapped by someone who was waging a vendetta against the *News of the World* was strengthened on the Thursday night by an anonymous letter that was pushed through the letter box of the *Hornsey*

Journal, a local paper covering the North London area. Hornsey is close to where Mrs. McKay's own letter had been posted the previous day. The new letter arrived just before the newspaper office was closing for the night. Written in block capitals, it was illiterate and full of misspellings. It said:

I am writing to your newspaper corse it don't try to corrupt young people like the News of the World does. Why should that rotten organisation worry that I might murder Mrs. McKay? They don't worry very much about all the kids' souls they murder with their evil pens. They pay out hundreds of thousands of pounds to no good girls to write their rotten stories so why shouldn't they pay me for not murdering Mrs. McKay?
I lost my twelve year old daughter corse she was influenced by all the money those dirty girls got paid for telling everyone about it. And now my girl is missing and the last I heard about her she was living with niggers like that —— was and she went with married men to. She got VD three times and the last I heard of her was three months ago. She may be lying dead somewhere for all I know so if Mr. McKay chose to aid and abet in the corruption of my child and lots of other children then he shouldn't complain or expect me to care what happens to his wife who lives off his filthy earned money. A million pounds won't really compensate me for the loss of my darling little girl but it wasn't me who asked for it.
—— the permissive society —— all the newspapers that encourage it.

The letter, which got a wide circulation the next day, was unsigned. On the back, the anonymous writer made a further claim: "P.S.—I will let Mrs. McKay go if the *News of the World* and the *Sun* publikly announce that they will not corrupt our kids any more by printing all that filth."
Thus that day, the third since Mrs. McKay vanished, was ending with a mass of speculation. By this time, both in private and in public, the police had become much more willing to accept that she was Britain's first kidnap victim. At a press conference on the Thursday, Smith said that there was "every

reason" to think that she was being held under duress by more than one person. It was the letter which had done most to convince him: "One would have to guard her," he explained, "while someone else posted it."

Few people doubted that the letter had been written by Mrs. McKay. The only suspicion that still existed was that it might have been sent deliberately to mislead the police and her family. But this was thought extremely unlikely. As a result of the taped telephone calls from M3, which the detectives had listened to closely a number of times, Smith now thought they were dealing with a gang of coloured men. From the sound of the voice, it was presumed that they were Jamaicans.

But despite the positive change in the thinking of detectives on the spot, it was not shared by all their superiors at Scotland Yard. On Thursday, a senior policeman had visited St. Mary House and generally nosed around the case. After a few hours, he accused Smith of wasting time and men; he thought it just another missing woman case.

Although their early extreme scepticism had now been abandoned, the police still had to continue to follow up all lines of enquiry: as yet, nothing was certain. This meant that on Thursday night, a team of Wimbledon detectives spent over six hours at St. Mary House checking all Mrs. McKay's personal correspondence, and also cross-questioning Alick about the holiday resorts which the couple had visited together. To him, it looked depressingly as if they were still working under the assumption that his wife had left of her own accord.

The situation was helped by the presence of Alick's son, Ian, and his young wife Lesley, who had arrived that morning from Australia. Aged twenty-seven, Ian worked as a marketing executive with the Hamlyn publishing group. He first heard the news of his mother's disappearance when reporters rang him at his office. He immediately decided that there was no alternative but to fly to London. "The only place I could be was with the family," he said. When he landed at Heathrow Airport, bronzed from the Australian sun, Ian was met by two of the detectives working on the case and driven straight to Arthur Road in a police car. During the hour-long journey, he was thoroughly briefed on all that had happened so far. Although it may not have been immediately realised, he was to prove the key to establishing a rapport between the police and the family. At the same time, his arrival was going to cause friction with some of those already installed at Arthur Road.

That night, with St. Mary House still the centre of concerted police activity, Alick and Dyer were even less convinced that the authorities were approaching the problem of rescuing Muriel in the right and most efficient way. As their despair mounted, they became keener than ever to see some action. The waiting reporters were conscious that something was afoot in the house, and long after midnight, they were assured by Dyer, "We shall have some news at noon today."

But this promise was to prove yet another example of the police and family working at cross purposes. The next morning, much to the journalists' disappointment, it was announced without explanation that the press conference had been cancelled. "We have nothing to tell the Press," said a police spokesman. It was becoming painfully obvious that something would have to be done to restore harmony between the two sides.

4
THE LONG HARD SEARCH

Friday, 2nd January

ALL FLEET STREET and Scotland Yard seemed to be encamped at St. Mary House. If the police were "in occupation" inside, the press were the besiegers, their camp the pavement in Arthur Road and, when they could get past the police guard at the gates, the gravel driveway.

Inside, all the family were now sharing the job of answering the incessantly ringing phone. Ian's presence was both a tonic and a source of some debate over the still-prickly issue of how far they should subjugate their efforts to the police needs.

Ian slept on after his flight from Australia the previous day but was wakened soon after Smith and Guiver arrived to discuss the situation. The police were still sore at the publication of the first ransom letter. Together Smith and Guiver had been to the Yard to discuss the problem of over-publicity with the Assistant Commissioner in charge of crime, Peter Brodie. They were still convinced that the McKays, acting from the best of motives, were hampering the police by courting publicity as the best method of getting Muriel returned safely.

Guiver emphasised to the family that they had not helped matters by telling the press they had enlisted the help of the Dutch medium Croiset. Now the McKays were likely to be inundated with offers of aid from other clairvoyants, which meant the phone would be further burdened with extraneous callers. What even Guiver did not then fully appreciate was the volume of interest the case had aroused, both in Britain and abroad. As a result, thousands of police man-hours were to be consumed following up "clues" which arrived at the house by phone, letter and through personal callers who had seen Mrs. McKay in tea leaves, crystal balls, and Tarot cards. In the words of the investigating squad based at St. Mary House, "The McKays were willing to try anything. If an Indian fakir had come along with a magic carpet they would have climbed aboard." Privately, the detectives at St. Mary House were highly embarrassed at the use of such unorthodox means, and they were coming in for some snide humour among their colleagues at the Yard.

Guiver, as tactfully as he could put it, asked the family to leave all future press publicity in the hands of the Yard Press Bureau, a public relations department whose aim is to act as the link between the detective and the journalist. The men who work for it are for the most part ex-journalists or civil servants with wide experience of police administration: the Yard's head of public relations is Bob Gregory, previously with Schweppes. But the Press Bureau does not have the easiest of lives; it often finds itself caught in the crossfire between the detective, who has an innate suspicion of the press, and the journalist denied the most trivial information. Andrew Henderson was the Bureau's District Liaison Officer (popularly and rather unfairly known in Fleet Street crime circles as "Don't Let On") who had been brought in to Wimbledon police station and to Arthur Road to try to co-ordinate the information reaching the newspapers.

Guiver's plea to the family succeeded in restoring some control to the police; previously the situation had threatened to get out of hand and wreck the whole investigation. In the police mind the newspapers had caused incalculable damage by disclosing too much too early, thus jamming the St. Mary House telephone by exciting public attention.

The press, on the other hand, were suspicious of the police actions. By that first week-end it appeared to the newspapers that there was no firm evidence that it was a kidnapping. The police appeared to have played down the importance of the one million pounds ransom demand call and seemed reluctant to read overmuch into Mrs. McKay's letter. So why the fuss over a "missing woman" case?

Some critics unkindly recalled the other disappearing woman, Mrs. Dawn Jones, a neighbour of the McKays from a less exclusive area of Wimbledon, a new Greater London Council housing estate. She had gone in even more puzzling circumstances, yet the Yard hierarchy had not rushed down day after day in their chauffeur-driven official cars. Was it the power of the people involved, the press barons? Was the Yard jumping because the Home Office was interested? And was the Home Secretary James Callaghan interested because he didn't want Fleet Street writing long editorials about the inefficiency of the police?

To be fair to the McKays, they had done nothing to stir the political pot. But the implications of their involvement were such that the police, being sensitive to criticism and an organisation with a civil service mind, had to act in order to cover themselves from possible future criticism.

Guiver conceded to the family the power to continue to make press and television statements, as long as they were first vetted by the Press Bureau in consultation with Smith. Both David Dyer and Ian McKay made brief appearances on the doorstep at Arthur Road on the Friday. Dyer, when asked about the many telephone calls, said he thought the criminals were trying to play on their nerves. "Whoever has got her, I want them to know this family isn't going to crack up."

On behalf of Alick McKay, his son Ian tried to scotch the rumours still circulating that Alick and Muriel had had disagreements about going back to their native Australia. The police had considered this angle but talks with Diane, reinforced by Ian's appraisal, had by now ruled it out. So Ian told the waiting journalists, "Both Alick McKay and his wife wish to continue to make their permanent home in England where they have lived for thirteen years."

At almost the same moment, the phone in the lounge at St. Mary House was ringing. A man's voice told Alick McKay that if he wanted his wife back home he had to find £500. The pay-off was to be later that night on platform five at Wimbledon railway station. McKay, with the money in a suitcase, was to meet the 5:20 P.M. train from Waterloo and wait until he saw his contact, who would be standing on the platform writing on a newspaper. There had been other calls demanding money but this was the first to talk about a meeting. Alick, his hopes raised by the contact, wanted to go himself. But Smith would not countenance the idea of McKay or any other civilian for that matter, going in person to the meeting place.

"No outsiders." It was a theme that was to recur throughout the case. The McKays were willing to go along with the kidnappers' orders; the police were just as determined they should stay away from physical contact with the criminals. Guiver and Smith had succeeded in persuading the family to concede full control; though the McKays' motives were unimpeachable, they were too vulnerable emotionally and might well lose their grip when faced with the kidnappers. Beyond the arrest itself was the question of court evidence and a conviction. A policeman's objectivity during the moments of arrest, his observations of what was done and said, far outweighed, in Smith's mind, the value of having the real Alick McKay on number five platform.

Once McKay had seen the wisdom of this view, he willingly supplied Minors and Smith with hats and coats from his own wardrobe. Then the two police officers left the house to keep the rendezvous with the man from the Waterloo train. Even here the police were bedevilled in their efforts to keep the meeting secret. A local journalist who saw them leaving the house followed them to the railway station. He saw Minors, wearing a fur hat, standing among the rush-hour crowds in the station hallway with a suitcase by his side. It contained about £150 in cash raised by the McKays in a pool of the contents of their wallets; underneath were plain sheets of paper cut to size.

Smith walked down onto the platform and watched the train pull in. When the commuter crowds had thinned out he saw a young man standing on the platform scribbling with a ballpoint pen on a newspaper. Smith went up and spoke to the youth. A few moments later the policeman and William Alexander Peat, a nineteen-year-old waiter, were on their way to Wimbledon police station. It was all a hoax; Smith had the task of breaking the news at St. Mary House later that night that they were no nearer finding Muriel McKay.

On the Saturday morning Peat, who lived in a bed-sitter in Warwick Road, Earls Court, London, appeared before the local magistrates and was remanded in custody, charged with attempting to obtain £500 from Alick McKay by deception. (Peat was later to be fined £100 with the alternative of three months in a detention centre. He apologised in court to McKay for the distress he had caused. Peat, it turned out, was something of a romantic: he believed he was acting in the best "urban guerrilla" traditions of Che Guevera, the South American revolutionary.)

By this time the Scotland Yard forensic science laboratory had come up with a fingerprint impression on the first letter written by Mrs. McKay. That it was not hers was proved by matching the print with some which had been taken from her bedroom. The scientists had also found a palm print on the *People* newspaper screwed up by Alick when he arrived home on the Monday evening. Both were checked with the criminal record files but neither "twin" was discovered.

The police had taken away examples of Mrs. McKay's handwriting to compare them with the ransom note. Graphology is as yet a less-recognised science than finger-printing in the forensic world and is a lengthy process. So far Smith had not been able to get definite confirmation that the writing was the same; for the time being he had to accept Alick McKay's word that the letter had been written by his wife.

The amount of routine background work was already substantial. There seemed no hope of tracing the ownership of the bill-hook, the bale of twine, or the Elastoplast. All that could be done was to enquire among local shopkeepers to see if they remembered selling any such articles. It was a long shot and it did not come off. The bill-hook was quite alien to the character of a London suburb like Wimbledon; the bale of twine, like the knife, suggested the countryside rather than densely populated S.W.19. Sales of sticking-plaster were so commonplace that there seemed little chance of pin-pointing an isolated purchase.

Descriptions of the jewellery Mrs. McKay had been wearing were circulated to shops, while underworld contacts were asked if they had heard of attempts to dispose of the missing items. There was always the chance that the criminals, unable to resist the temptation, would attempt to raise cash for the jewellery even though they would be putting themselves in danger. But even this trail petered out; the jewellery was never seen again. Logical and illogical by turns, the kidnappers had obviously realised the perils attendant on such a move.

Saturday, 3rd January

By that first weekend, St. Mary House had become something of a national curiosity, with Arthur Road almost blockaded by press and sight-seers. Despite the bitter cold, there were upwards of forty journalists maintaining their watch throughout the day and most of the night; American television cameras turned up, then the French who spoke hardly a word of English but who simply pointed their lens in the direction the crowd was heading. The French television crew were disappointed at the bourgeois atmosphere of St. Mary House. Perhaps they had expected to find a press baron's chateau more in the style of William Randolph Hearst, for they soon moved off, found a house nearby that was more fitted to the story, and photographed it instead, for the information of their viewers.

Inside the house, matters were a little less tense, though the perpetual ringing of the telephone tended to make everybody jumpy. Smith had succeeded in getting closer to the family now. They were impressed by the shrewd way he had dealt with the Peat case and were now accepting the fact that his priorities were the same as theirs, even if the police methods appeared to lack the urgency that they felt the situation required.

Alick McKay had agreed to play along with the superintendent by exaggerating his own ill-health and that of his wife. McKay had suffered badly from his wife's disappearance but his general constitution was strong. The police however felt he should be kept out of the way as much as he could, not answer the phone unless absolutely necessary, and appear in public as little as possible. With McKay's approval the police put round the story that his health was much worse than in fact it was. Again at Smith's prompting, McKay agreed to give a bleak impression of his wife's condition. She was, in fact quite healthy: her private physician, Dr. Tadeus Markowitz, had examined her two days before her disappearance and had found her in good health although she had suffered for some years from arthritis.

But Smith and Guiver had argued to Alick McKay the case for a "false diagnosis": if during the course of his talks with M3 he stressed the need for Muriel to receive vitamin injections, this might force them to call in a doctor or go to a chemist. Scotland Yard had already put out a confidential bulletin asking to be notified if particular drugs or medicines were sought by a patient who had previously had no need of them.

It was one of the few occasions in the early stages of the case when the police were able to take the initiative. Tragically the ploy failed, probably because Mrs. McKay was already dead.

On Saturday evening, Smith held one of his press conferences at Wimbledon police station; he was still inclined to be amiable even after four days and nights on his feet. Yes, evidence still pointed to the fact that Mrs. McKay had been forcibly abducted; no, there had been no more letters from her; the phone calls were continuing and the daily post bag at St. Mary House still carried a mixture of abuse and sympathy.

But was it a kidnapping? "How do we know?" Smith answered, now a little terse and harassed. "We've never had one before." If she had been abducted, he asked, what was preventing the person holding her from coming forward?

What about the "rusty meat-cleaver"? (Bill-hook, sickle: many names were used to describe it during the enquiry.) To the outsiders it seemed of tremendous significance. Smith said guardedly that it "appeared to be alien to the house"; but then wasn't one bill-hook like another, he added, appearing to minimise its significance.

It was left to Henderson, the Press Bureau DLO, to field the rest of the bowling. Were pictures of the bill-hook or the jewellery ready for issuing to the papers yet? No. Why was the Yard making exceptional efforts in this case? They were not; every suspected abduction was treated as a major enquiry. It was the prominence of the family that was bringing the police work under such close scrutiny.

It was a surmise that was close to the truth. Yet there were grounds for scepticism: the pictures of the bill-hook and the jewellery were not given to the press until the following week, rather tardily in the view of some people. It did not suggest that the police were driven on by any frenzy to apply a solution to the mystery. After the case Commander Guiver took this issue of the police making "exceptional efforts" a bit further when he said, "I am convinced that there would not have been anything like the interest even if, say, the son of a famous film star had been kidnapped. It was the McKays' press background. For the first three or four days they genuinely believed publicity would bring her back."

An hour or so after the police conference, attention switched back to the house when it was announced that Alick McKay was ready to talk to the press. The journalists had been allowed past the police watch-dogs on the double gates and into the drive. There they heard with dismay the news that Alick was not well enough to stand up to the rigours of a mass question-and-answer session: he would see only a reporter and photographer from the Press Association and the story would be circulated to all newspapers via them.

When the men from the news agency were eventually admitted to the house, McKay was sitting in the living room in striped pyjamas, slippers, and a maroon, flower-patterned dressing-gown. On a table beside him were pictures of his wife and children—a very normal smiling family group. Ian McKay, the daughters, and the rest of the family left the room when the reporter and photographer entered.

McKay read a prepared statement which had been drawn up with police guidance: there were to be no questions. He looked tired and low in spirits and took a tablet washed down with water before starting. The interview, he said, was being given without his doctor's permission. He had suffered a coronary the previous year and although he had been making progress "recent events have brought about complications in my condition."

Reading slowly he said, "I have now received many calls and letters regarding my wife. So far I have received no demand specific enough for me to believe the demands are genuine. Nor, since the letter I received from Muriel on Wednesday, have I had any further news of her or from her.

"I ask whoever is holding Muriel to get in touch with me

immediately and let me know exactly what they want. If it is money, then I must know how and where it can be exchanged for my wife.

"In order to be certain I am dealing with the person who is holding Muriel I must have positive proof that she is safe.

"To whoever is holding her: Do you realise, whoever you are, how dangerous will be the state of my wife's health if she doesn't get the drugs she needs quickly?"

It was the most successful press coup the police had yet achieved. In one manoeuvre they had both got across the impression that Alick was ill—it was at their suggestion that he wore the pyjamas and dressing-gown—and that his wife needed medical attention urgently. They had also conveyed the idea that the kidnappers must make contact: the next move now lay with the other side.

Alick McKay was certainly not short of friends in his time of need. On the Saturday, among a stream of callers, came Stafford Somerfield, editor of the *News of the World*, who was soon to lose his job. And Lord Robens, whom McKay had got to know well through business committees they had both sat on, issued a statement saying it was monstrous that rumours had got about of a vendetta against the McKay family. The then chairman of the National Coal Board said, "If those responsible for this disgraceful act knew this devoted couple as I do, they would know them to be amongst the kindest and most charitable people who have devoted their lives to public causes." (Proof of the respect with which McKay was held was later to come in the shape of an offer from an Australian newspaper tycoon to loan as much money as was necessary to meet the kidnappers' demands. It was said that by the end of the whole affair Alick McKay, through the good offices of friends, could probably have raised the whole one million pounds.)

While the early editions of the Sunday newspapers were all prominently featuring the case, the *Sunday Telegraph* was running a story that owed much to foresight or good guess work. It said that the police now privately believed Mrs. McKay had been murdered. Whatever the personal views of the Scotland Yard men associated with the case—and there were several different versions at that stage, according to which man was voicing his thoughts—the Press Bureau hurriedly denied the suggestion she was dead. "We are still hopeful that she will be found safe and well. We are treating this case as one of abduction" (and not murder, they implied). The *Sunday Telegraph* story may have been premature but it certainly anticipated a view the police themselves were to take a fortnight later.

Next day, members of the family attended service at the neighbouring church in Arthur Road where prayers were said for Mrs. McKay's safe return. And for the police, although it was a Sunday, the job of manning the telephone and the tape-recorder, of guarding the house and its occupants went on unchecked. The men at the house were working three eight-hour shifts; they would be relieved by colleagues from Wimbledon who, although not engaged on the enquiry, could be spared from other work for a couple of hours.

Around them the family life somehow struggled on with Diane Dyer and Jennifer Burgess doing the cooking and helping Mrs. Nightingale, the domestic, to keep the house straight. It was not easy with so many strangers trampling through it, even though the policemen were careful not to leave behind muddy foot-prints and always took away their sandwich papers.

One man who spent many days in the house in this strange atmosphere said of the characters there, "Ian Burgess was mostly sitting by the fire reading newspapers, a quiet, easy-going personality whose attitude was 'stop worrying and leave it to the police.'" David Dyer, a bundle of energy, was always rushing all over the place. The daughters somehow managed to contain their distress by busying themselves with the chores and then there was Ian who was to have a harmonising effect.

"Understandably there were times when friction developed. You couldn't expect anything else with a family brought together in such circumstances. Some members of the family were upset over the amount of press publicity; others thought it was the only answer. Ian McKay and David Dyer both thought that theirs was the best method of getting through to the kidnappers. You couldn't dispute their right in the circumstances to act as they saw fit. David, who is quite a dynamic businessman, used to having control of a situation, had a Sherlock Holmes approach to the case while Ian was all for the police doing the job."

And Alick McKay? It is perhaps one of the most bizarre features of the whole case that for many days the police regarded him as their major suspect. (This was mentioned by Ian McKay during the court proceedings.) The more he appeared to be whole-heartedly co-operating with them, the more it could have been a ploy to put them off the track. After all, according to police reasoning, when a woman goes missing in suspicious circumstances, they immediately look for the man in the background (the *cherchez la femme* theory in reverse). Here they were only putting long experience to the test; experience was all they had to go on at that time, a question of matching known behaviour in other crimes with what might have happened here.

Gradually the probabilities began to point suspicion away from Alick. There was never a precise moment at which the detectives could say, "He is innocent." But once the M3 phone calls began coming in thick and fast in the latter half of January, the police were satisfied he was utterly guiltless.

For the third time in a week, the police searched the house wondering if Mrs. McKay had got lost right under their noses. (If this sounds ridiculous, it isn't. In one London East End murder case, the victim, a young girl, was hidden behind a false wall at the back of a wardrobe; in another case, a young boy climbed into a trunk and was found dead only after the police had searched the entire house three times.) At St. Mary House they once more poked about the garage, climbed into the loft, inspected the garden for evidence of recent digging and looked into sheds in surrounding gardens.

The index files kept at Wimbledon police station already amounted to many hundreds of statements: from neighbours, from well-meaning members of the public who had reported seeing Mrs. McKay in all manner of situations (on a London-Glasgow express; being led blindfolded by two men across fields at nearby Roehampton). The freezup prevented ponds on Wimbledon common being dragged for several weeks: the ice on top of the water was several inches thick. Even the All-England Lawn Tennis Club, a short distance from the McKay home, was searched.

There was also a report from the Sheffield police who had been to visit a manufacturer of bill-hooks. When the bill-hook found at St. Mary House was described to him, the maker had said this particular implement was peculiar to the Hertfordshire area: it was of a type sold and used around Bishop's Stortford. Enquiries in shops there took the investigation no further. It seemed that every farmer and gardener in the district had one. If the police had only known, at that moment they were within a matter of miles of the kidnappers!

Tuesday, 6th January

By now a week had gone by and still the police were utterly perplexed. Men with vast experience admitted they had never come across anything like it. Scotland Yard's Assistant Commissioner (Crime), Peter Brodie, called a conference with Smith and Guiver. First they reviewed the evidence, scanty as it was; then they examined the theories and possibilities and finally discussed where they were to go from there.

The third issue was the crucial one: were the police now simply to treat it as a missing person case—which would mean withdrawing the detectives and handing it back to the uniformed branch—or was it to be escalated into a major enquiry? Guiver and Smith were in no doubt that some crime had been committed; they were only slightly less certain that Mrs. McKay had not gone off freely. Whether or not one believed the one million pounds demand or the letter, they could not be ignored as evidence that some offence had been committed. Then there were the "foreign" objects found at the house and the missing £25 and the jewellery. Both men were convinced there was every point in stepping up the activity. Brodie concurred and went back to Scotland Yard to put the Commissioner, Sir John Waldron, in the picture.

That day, 6th January, every Metropolitan policeman was issued with Mrs. McKay's description and pictures were prepared for display on police "Wanted and Missing" boards throughout Britain. Interpol was also circulated with details for onward transmission to other national forces, particularly the Australian police. Again, there was to be criticism that these steps were taken rather late in the day (the pictures of

Mrs. McKay were not posted until the following Monday, thirteen days after her disappearance). If the police had been in possession then of some of the evidence later accumulated, they would certainly have acted much sooner. But something like twenty adults go missing in Britain every day; giving priority to Mrs. McKay would have redoubled the criticism already voiced that their actions were influenced by the standing of the personalities involved.

Guiver had brought in a permanent squad of thirty detectives for full-time duty on the case. Some he had to borrow from other divisions. "That was alright until they were wanted back again. Then it's a question of who's the stronger man, me or Commander Bloggs. If I can win the argument then I keep the men; if I lose they go back. You can understand the other man's point of view; I've been in just the same position. For weeks you see your men kicking their heels on someone else's enquiry while your case-load is growing and growing. So eventually you get them back—and at that moment the other enquiry blows up into something big."

The thirty detectives were broken up into three-man groups working under Minors, who was Smith's "first lieutenant." There was even more need for secrecy in this instance than in most major enquiries. The "cell" structure of the team helped; each group would know only the details of its own work. Smith and Minors alone had the overall picture. Guiver, responsible for a much larger area of south and southwest London than Wimbledon alone, would look in each day for progress reports. "Two heads are always better than one. I might spot something Smith had overlooked. Nobody minds." Then, when necessary, Guiver would put Brodie in the picture and finally the Assistant Commissioner (Crime) would pass on a progress bulletin to Sir John Waldron at the Yard. The higher it got, the less the emphasis on routine, the more on the general outline.

A number of senior detectives at the Yard were casting covetous eyes on the McKay case now that it had escalated into a major investigation. Policemen are no less possessed of the foible of ambition than their fellow men. Brodie had made up his mind from the start that Smith, the man "in possession" down at V. Division, was to run the affair, but there were precedents for sending in men from the Yard's C.1 department, where a question of co-ordination of effort between several areas became necessary. (John DuRose, when on the Murder Squad, had been sent to Shepherds Bush to centralise all enquiries in the London nudes murders in the early 1960s. But that decision had been taken because the murders had taken place in different divisions; so far the McKay case did not look like spilling outwards from Wimbledon and V. Division in the same manner.)

This did not, however, stop a certain amount of professional jealousy creeping in. As one Yard detective explained, "You will always have the type of man hanging around, trying to catch the chief's eye if there's a big job on. If you get in on a really big job—like the Train Robbery—and it's a success from a police point of view, it might help your chances of promotion. And let's face it, some policemen are publicists: they enjoy the limelight and the glamour." The jealousy was not lessened by the fact that Brodie, Guiver, and Smith were all keeping very quiet about the case. A policeman is no more and no less of a gossip than anybody else: it's just that he's usually got a lot more to say. So many secrets had already been exposed that any more careless talk, whether at the Yard or at Wimbledon, would make the investigation almost impossible.

Guiver, as the senior rank in the case, was to encounter some of this petty resentment. With a man of less strength of character it might have affected the balance of the police team. But Guiver is a man of wide experience who, with Brodie's blessing, was able to put absolute trust in Smith's field generalship. Moreover, Guiver, now security adviser to the Grand Metropolitan chain of hotels, retired from Scotland Yard soon after the Hoseins were under lock and key; his formal notice of retirement at pensionable age had gone in to the Commissioner long before the case first raised its head.

Smith had arrived at Wimbledon only a couple of months before on his promotion from Detective Superintendent in W. Division (Balham and Tooting). At forty-nine, this Burnley-born man, who had been in the R.A.F. during the war, was to find that his first major crime in the public sense was to be one that would go down in the annals of crime history. He is a stocky, perky man with the policeman's unrivalled ability for sharp, abrasive humour coupled with the capacity to encapsulate long arguments into one pithy expletive.

Minors, Smith's number two, carried a large share of the responsibility for the day-to-day progress in the case. Taller than Smith, never lacking in self-confidence, Minors too was an R.A.F. man in World War II.

The third man who formed the core of the Wimbledon team was the operations controller, Detective Sergeant Parker, forty-three, a native of Brighton. It was Parker who, in the words of a colleague, "had the dirty job: sorting the wheat from the chaff—and there was a lot of chaff. They made a funny old trio: Smith and Minors up front and Parker—who's about six-foot-one and towers over the two of them—back at the ranch."

One of the Wimbledon teams had the most hilarious experience in a case that was never very strong on humour. On 12th January, a telephone caller instructed Diane Dyer to travel on a certain South London bus route with a case containing £5,-000. When she saw a parked car flashing its lights, she was to get off at the next stop. Detective Sergeant White was chosen to impersonate Diane and dressed up in a wig, head-scarf, mini-skirt, and tights. At stops along the route White was discreetly joined by two colleagues, posing respectively as a garage-worker and a train-driver.

Before the bus had gone very far, the woman conductor had noticed White and seen through his disguise. In her disgust at the antics of this obvious transvestite she stopped the bus and rang the local police. It was several minutes before White could convince the sceptical occupants of a police patrol car that he was dressed in drag for a legitimate reason.

The hoaxer in this particular case, although he was never caught, showed himself to be a man with a conscience. He rang the house again the next day to apologise for not keeping the rendezvous and explained that first he had to get money to buy a car so that he could fetch Mrs. McKay and deliver her up. This time he asked Diane Dyer to catch a train to Catford and at a spot where she saw a bonfire alight by the railway line she was to throw out £200 for the purchase of the car. The police decided the whole idea was a hoax and the caller's proposition was ignored. The same man phoned again the following day explaining that both calls had been hoaxes, apologised for the trouble and distress he had caused and rang off, never to be heard from again.

Another ransom demand, this time by letter to the McKay home, said that on receipt of £2,000 Mrs. McKay would be returned "within a few hours." For once a rendezvous was arranged and detectives, disguised as factory-workers, kept watch on a public toilet outside Stratford underground station in East London. They arrested Roy Edward Roper, twenty-six, of Leytonstone, London. Roper was later jailed for three years on two charges connected with the £2,000 demand.

The police decision to increase their efforts in the case went some way toward satisfying critics who felt there had been too little urgency in the early days. One man close to the McKay family circle commented, "Once the police had made up their minds it was a kidnapping, you could not quarrel with their efforts. But it had taken them a week to get rid of the idea that she had not gone off on her own. And we now know that those first days were vital: Muriel died in that time. Alick kept assuring them she had no reason to disappear like that. It seemed to go in one ear and out of the other."

Friday, 9th January

Other people too were asking what the police were doing. On Friday, 9th January, an extraordinary article appeared in the London *Evening News*. What was so unusual about it was the forthright way in which it cast doubt on the efficacy of the police work. Contrary to common belief, the British press does not easily resort to "police bashing," particularly when an investigation is a continuing one; if anything, our papers tend to be too unquestioning of police methods. Not only was this article out of character, it caught the bewilderment felt by all concerned with the case. The paper called it "The Case That Does Not Add Up" and said the police were no closer to an accurate explanation for Mrs. McKay's disappearance than when they were first called in.

After reviewing the progress of the case so far, the paper
went on, in terms more suited to an editorial than a news
report:

Mr. McKay, who is convinced that his wife is being held
prisoner by someone, is confident she was not suffering any
emotional strain.
But could she have been?
Early in the investigation the police appeared to think so.
McKay's decision to ignore his own ill-health and join the
News of the World rather than return to his native Aus-
tralia had disappointed her, they said.
In the words of a spokesman, "The falling through of her
return to Australia is known to have caused Mrs. McKay a
certain amount of concern."
The police say that Mrs. McKay "took the burglary* badly"
—it may have preyed on her mind.
But the family and her friends in the Wimbledon Senior
Wives' Fellowship say that she showed no signs of distress.
But if the police are convinced that Mrs. McKay merely
wandered off they have given no clear hint of it, either publicly or in private.
The intensive nature of their enquiries contrasts markedly
with the investigation into the disappearance late last year
of Mrs. McKay's Wimbledon neighbour, Mrs. Dawn Jones,
who, finally, was found dead in Scotland, an apparent
suicide.
But the whole police procedure in the McKay case seems
odd. It was not until Monday of this week (5th January)
that they released pictures of the bill-hook which was found
at the house although they were known to be anxious to
trace anyone who might recognise it.
Nor did they release until the same day, pictures of Mrs.
McKay's jewellery which was absent from the house.
... and although photographs of Mrs. McKay have been
issued to the press, they will not be posted up in police

---

* The burglary three months before which led to the chain on the outer
door.

stations until next Monday—a fortnight after the disappearance.

... At one time the police denied they were making enquiries in Australia—although such enquiries would appear logical. The next day they confirmed the Australian police were assisting them.*

... And why has only part of the mysterious one million pounds ransom letter been released? There could have been many good reasons—it may have contained high-personal [sic] material. But no statement to this effect has been made.

The tenor of the *Evening News* article summed up the frustration of the family, the police, and the public at large who viewed the affair with a mixture of incredulity and unbounded curiosity. The police were in the unfamiliar role of being the shuttlecock in an investigation. On one side they were being accused of overreacting without evidence to justify such attention; on the other side they were being berated for not treating it as a major investigation. (In fact, by the time the *Evening News* article appeared, the crucial decision had been taken to regard it as a serious crime. But the press were not to know at the time: the Yard had no intention of unnecessarily fanning the publicity flames.)

On the Friday night, Alick McKay briefly went on television to appeal for proof that his wife was still alive. Since the letter from Muriel eight days before, there had not been one vestige of a "serious" contact. McKay, still looking pale and drawn, said his son Ian or his sons-in-law were prepared to meet anyone anywhere who could help to trace his wife. "I just can't understand why those holding Muriel have not contacted me recently."

As if in answer to this plea, a letter arrived next day, Saturday, at the *News of the World* offices, addressed "Personal and Urgent" to Stafford Somerfield, the paper's editor,

---

* This was not completely accurate. Scotland Yard had not contacted Australia: they were able to check from the British end that she had not left the country.

who after reading the contents immediately drove to Arthur Road. Smith and Alick McKay read the letter together. It said that when McKay arranged for the police to leave his home and was free to talk, the writer would telephone to give his instructions. One million pounds was to be collected on two occasions, half a million pounds at each rendezvous. If McKay co-operated, he would see his wife. If he failed to co-operate, "his wife will be disposed of." The writer said McKay could raise the money by borrowing it from friends (this was obviously in answer to McKay's earlier statements in the press that he had "nothing like one million pounds"). The letter added "immediate attention is important. He" [McKay] "is in no position to bargain."

The letter was on white writing paper with turquoise blue lines. A similar sheet of paper torn from an exercise book was found in Nizam's bedroom at Rooks Farm. Marks on this sheet matched with the ransom note: the tear line, the stapling and in particular an inverted "V" used as an insertion mark which had left an indent on the paper beneath. Even the words "St. Mary" (intended to be the name of the McKays' home) appeared to have gone through.

Several words in the letter were misspelt: "off" instead of "of," "existance" and "occassion." The letter was sent to the scientific laboratories the same day for print examination and photo-chemical analysis to try to establish the type of ink and paper that had been used. For the family and the detectives, it at least meant that an eight-day silence had been broken, though there was then no means of positively connecting the letter with the earlier phone calls: the one million pound demand was now public knowledge.

As if in explanation—almost apology—for the long silence, the letter writer said he had tried to ring St. Mary House several times but could not get through because the line was continually engaged. At that time Somerfield could not take the explanation seriously: when he showed the police the letter he found they were inclined to believe it. It bore out their contention that until publicity died down there would not be much chance of making any kind of arrangement.

On the same afternoon, Alick McKay made another statement to reporters at his home. The Press Bureau had asked for questions to be submitted in advance; they would not allow a general question-and-answer session. When several questions were deleted by the Yard DLO, an open row developed. Among those questions the Yard refused to allow Alick to answer were:

"Did you find a letter from your wife when you got home?"

"What do you think in retrospect happened that night?"

"How long was it before you telephoned the police?"

"Did you contact any relatives before you phoned the police?"

"Are you satisfied the police have told you everything?"

The third question was pressed at the news conference despite the Yard's reluctance, but before McKay could reply, the Press Bureau representative said, "I think it will be sufficient to say that you raised the alarm."

This further breach of press-police relations was not at all healed by a Yard statement later that night in answer to complaints from Fleet Street news desks. "There were certain questions that the family didn't wish to answer. There were others which should have been put to the police and not to the family and which the police did not wish answered as the information might have interfered with the investigation."

Looking back, one wonders why the Yard were being so obstructive when the questions could do little harm; certainly not when compared with what had already happened. There was no farewell letter from Mrs. McKay as the first question implied; McKay could only say what the police were already saying ("we are treating it as a major investigation"); there were rumours that McKay had taken an excessively long time to phone the police but evidence at the trial showed that he had rung the police within fifteen minutes of getting home and had not rung relatives first.

That left the question "Are you satisfied the police have told you everything?" McKay could only hazard a guess at such a question and he was scarcely likely to re-commence friction between the family and the police by saying, "No, I am not satisfied."

So, all in all, the questions were rather innocuous. It was once more a case of the Yard trying to stifle the excess of publicity—but only tending to make matters worse.

At the news conference, Alick McKay again told the journalists that the family were ready to make contact just as soon as the abductors named the place and the amount. Yes, certainly she had been abducted; she would not go off on her own like this. Countless times he had been asked that question and always he had given the same answer; it is a pity that some did not listen to him more closely earlier on.

In reply to the rumour that she had been taken away because of her husband's connections with the *News of the World,* McKay said, "I joined the group only a few days before Christmas and then only as a part-time director." His wife had been permitted no access to money since she left: their joint bank account had now been cancelled. Then he made an appeal to all the telephone pests to leave the McKays alone; there had been far too many phone calls, he said, singling out—possibly with prompting from the police—"an extreme number from spiritualists offering assistance."

It was perhaps an indelicate moment to pick out the mediums for police criticism. That day Croiset, the Dutch seer, had arrived in London and, accompanied by David Dyer, Eric Cutler, the family friend, and a *Daily Mail* journalist, was travelling round London trying to follow the route he thought Mrs. McKay had taken after being picked up at Arthur Road. Guiver was particularly unhappy at this; after the harmony Smith had carefully built up, the family were getting in the way again. "All this medium business: it wasted no end of time," Guiver said later.

Three totally unrewarding days followed. Guiver and Smith were now forced to consider the possibility that someone with a personal hatred of McKay was responsible. As Guiver explained, "We thought it might be some sick character who was trying to break Alick down. Not for money—because they weren't talking about ransom in terms that made any sense—but just as a sick kind of grudge. Or alternatively it might be someone with a warped dislike of the *News of the World.*"

The "Screws of the World," as it is popularly known in Fleet Street, is something of a national institution: like it or deplore its journalistic standards, you cannot ignore its influence. It is scarcely surprising then that such a paper, with a circulation in the region of six million, has its share of enemies. The Yard checked the threatening letters received by the paper over recent years, went through the lists of employees to see if there might be any with a grudge against the organisation, and even examined the paper's exposé files to see whom it had offended and who might retaliate by taking Mrs. McKay. The detectives also investigated McKay's business and personal background. From all these sources a number of names were noted and enquiries made: none filled the shoes of prospective kidnappers.

The *News of the World* had received dozens of telephone calls from ersatz kidnappers as well as more than a hundred letters since its connection with the McKay case had become public knowledge. On Wednesday, 14th January, Stafford Somerfield took a personal call in his office. The call would never have reached him but for a remarkable coincidence in the use of the code letter "M." Somerfield's secretary, told that the caller was "M," put him through on the editor's private phone without further question. Somerfield was on speaking terms with the head of the British Secret Service who, ever since its inception, had been known as "M." Somerfield picked up the phone and barked jovially down it, "What the hell do you want then?" He realised his mistake when a voice, apparently that of a coloured man, said he wanted to talk about "the McKay case; Mrs. McKay." The caller asked Somerfield if he had received a letter (the one which arrived on 10th January.) He again identified himself as "M" and then "M3." It was a short conversation: the instructions were "tell McKay to get a million. I have proof of Mrs. McKay's existence." When Somerfield asked M3 who he was, the man rang off.

Somerfield went straight to the McKay house. He told Smith he thought the voice was that of a coloured man, possibly a West Indian. On the tape-recorder, the police played back a number of conversations to him and on one M3 call Somerfield recognised the same voice.

Later that day, Alick McKay took a call from M3—their first audible contact with the family since January 1st, thirteen days before.

M3 told McKay: "You co-operate and you'll get your madam back."

McKay: "Thank you very much ... Can you tell me one

thing, has she had any of the drugs she needs, or medicines?"

Yes, she had, said M3, but the medical treatment was "costing a lot."

McKay: "Well, we want her as quickly as possible."

M3: "Okay, I'll contact you."

McKay and the policemen monitoring the call were in no doubt that it was the same voice as in the previous conversations with M3. Some sort of pattern was at last beginning to emerge, though there was too little as yet to point the police in any one direction.

For the first time in a crime investigation in his country, the police turned to the infant and as yet unproven science of voice-printing to try to discover M3's identity. That Scotland Yard was willing to move into uncharted fields was proof of their willingness to use any method to solve a case which was beyond their experience. But again a degree of scepticism first had to be overcome.

The Home Office runs a Scientific Advisory Council for the purpose of adapting the resources of the technological age to police work; its successes have included lightweight pocket radios for men on the beat and "optical telephones"—outsize binoculars with two-way receivers for transmitting messages by light waves. The Council is broken up into two sub-committees, Forensic Science and Equipment (the production of "hardware" such as cars and radios). Industry provides its experts to sit on these committees: Pilkington (glass), Rolls Royce (cars and engines), I.C.I. (paints and fibres), Dunlop (rubber). It was through this liaison, for instance, that the police recently learnt that the brand name of a piece of rubber left at the scene of a crime can be easily established. Yet there is an orthodoxy and conservatism inherent in the policeman's make-up that makes him suspicious of progress and change, perhaps because his job is principally the preservation of the *status quo*. One scientist who has worked closely with the police and the Home Office Scientific Advisory Council for some years said, "New ideas are being produced, but you have first got to overcome the reservations the British police have about untried methods."

The Home Office scientists had already briefly looked into the possibilities of voice-printing before the McKay case: they

Muriel McKay

Alick McKay faces the press in pyjamas and dressing gown.

Diane Dyer and Jennifer Burgess,
Mrs. McKay's daughters

Ian McKay and David Dyer talking to reporters

St. Mary House, Arthur Road, Wimbledon

Deputy Chief Superintendent Smith and Detective Inspector Minors after the Hoseins had been remanded in custody

Aerial view of Rooks Farm during the police search

ELASTOPLAST

BARCLAY CARD

RIPPED TELEPHONE

BALING TWINE

BILLHOOK

What Alick McKay saw when he opened his front door on Monday evening, 29th December, 1969. (The Barclay Card is a credit card issued by Barclays Bank.)

Artist's impressions of Arthur *(left)* and Nizam Hosein

Mrs. McKay's bedroom. A jewellery box in the open bureau drawer
appeared to have been disturbed.

The futile police search: on Wimbledon common...

...and later at Rooks Farm

had seen the results of ten years of research by the Bell Telephone Laboratories in America. Bell have found that voice spectrograms—to give them their proper title—are little "pictures" of a person's speech. The pictures are obtained by a machine that transcribes the sound of spoken words into graphed patterns of voice energy. Bell consider that the natural shape of a person's mouth, throat, and nasal cavities causes the voice energy to be concentrated into bands of frequencies. Efforts to disguise the voice would be futile because the identifying process depends upon the shape of the voice energy produced and not the sound.

Some scientists are of the belief that within two generations voice-prints may take their place beside finger-prints as unequivocal evidence of a person's identity. Anyone who has read Alexander Solzhenitsyn's novel *The First Circle* will remember the exhaustive account of attempts by Russian scientists to perfect a system of voice-printing during the final years of Stalin's life.

When Guiver told Brodie of the pattern the telephone calls were beginning to take—M3, a coloured man's voice, possibly a West Indian—the Assistant Commissioner (Crime) referred to the notes from the Home Office on voice-printing. The tapes of the M3 calls were sent by car to an acoustics laboratory at a provincial university. The head of the department, after studying the recordings, told the Yard that he too believed it was a West Indian voice, possibly with an Americanised accent. From that time the consensus of opinion among the Yard and Wimbledon detectives was that they were searching for four West Indians—four being the number who appeared to be involved in the crime: two abductors, one who had driven the car and the fourth, the organiser.

Unaccountably, even this story of the police looking for four "Jamaicans" found its way into the papers. So too did disclosures that the police had now discovered new clues in the 1st January letter from Mrs. McKay, and that she had now been murdered by her kidnappers. The suggestion of clues in the letter angered the Yard, who said it implied they had overlooked something the first time round. (They had not missed anything, but then, Scotland Yard is always sensitive to suggestions that it is fallible. One Metropolitan police detective concerned with the case who was then based on division and not at the Yard said, "The Yard believes that it is the 'cream' of the police service. It is a myth which has been created by themselves and by the press as a source of good copy. It is a myth which is fast disappearing.")

Saturday and Sunday, 17th and 18th January

By the third week-end of the enquiry, as the police had been avidly hoping, publicity and the attendant public appetite for the story had at last begun to wane. It was a story which had gone all round the world and the men at the center of the speculation had never known, nor wanted to know again, the like of it. Guiver was emphatic about the harmful effects of publicity: "At first it made our job impossible: later on just difficult. It could be that because of the interest generated, the kidnappers were forced to a point of no return with their victim. We could scarcely make a move without them" [the press] "following us and watching us. They were at the house or outside the station day and night, scrutinising everyone who came and went." But how were embarrassing leaks getting into the papers? The *Evening Standard* on 19th January carried a story saying, "One detective told a London news-agency early today, 'We have received information that she is being held by a gang somewhere in London.'" Scotland Yard countered with yet another denial, this time that such a statement had ever been made. Despite this, some people concerned with the affair feel that the press were not the only party who were less than wholly discreet.

Guiver conceded that such things *might* happen: policemen are only human after all; "but it is the press who create this situation. It wasn't just the reporters' fault. They were being pushed further and further by their editors. The reputable men, the established crime reporters, were all right. But we were being messed around by the freelances, many of them down at Wimbledon on lineage* for the day, living on what they could feed to a paper to justify their expenses. The most outrageous stories were getting into print."

---

* Payment according to the number of lines the paper uses.

Specialist journalists have a number of associations, among them motoring, industry, football—and crime. Being a member of the Crime Reporters' Association has certain advantages, including the chance to get to know policemen on first-name terms. But as with all specialist groups there is a tendency to "play ball" with the police in order not to upset good contacts.

Apart from the CRA men down at Wimbledon there were also many general news reporters, men who will turn their hand to any kind of story. These were the journalists who were getting in the hair of the police and making the job of the Press Bureau a thankless one. As one of the crime reporters admitted, "We in the CRA think we are gods and we are the only people who know anything about crime in the press world. When the general reporters come in they are immediately ostracised by the CRA men. Yet these people are usually better diggers than we are because they operate in a less rigid manner. They embarrass us by getting some good stories and as a result a feud blows up. In the middle you've got the Press Bureau man who is busy denying what one half know to be a fact.

"A lot of information Smith and Minors had certainly wasn't for the public ear, otherwise it could have harmed the enquiry. As a result the Yard bureau men like Henderson, while being privy to a lot of information, were not empowered to release it. At the front door they were refusing to talk about a disclosure that had already slipped out of the back door."

Routine crime does not take a holiday just because the police are otherwise engaged. People were asking during the McKay case how the priorities of an investigation were calculated. Were complainants in less glamorous crimes getting less attention because of the concentration of manpower at St. Mary House?

In manpower terms, estimating the needs of a crime investigation is of necessity a very imprecise art. What may start out as just a puff of smoke may develop like a bush fire. There is no such yardstick as profitability: the most that can be done is to leave it to the judgment of the senior man on the spot. There are however a number of "floating" brigades not pinned down to a particular territory who can be called in to supplement manpower needs. Smith was to use all these resources: the Flying Squad, the Commando Squad (a unit of uniformed men ready for anything from field digging to riot duty), the Regional Crime Squad, the provincial mobile detective units, and the Home Counties regional crime squad, known as the "Home and Colonial."

Even so, taking Smith, Minors, and other detectives away from unfinished enquiries did mean some diminution of attention to routine events such as housebreaking and robbery. One Wimbledon officer commented, "They took the best for the McKay job and the rest of us were overloaded. What was normally a ten to twelve hours day became twelve hours compulsory. We were doing two men's work. Other cases got attended to but with the best will in the world you can't expect a man to do his best in these circumstances: nor can the public get the service they pay for."

Guiver and Smith had been convinced for some days now that Mrs. McKay was dead. They felt it was time to tell the family their fears, both for their own sakes and as a further unifying factor in the attempt to catch the common enemy. The McKays listened quietly as Smith explained the process of reasoning which had brought the police to this conclusion. Only Alick McKay, while he did not argue with the logic of Smith's case, clung to the hope that his wife was still alive somewhere. As Guiver said later, "Alick never really accepted what we said. He went on hoping. But at the same time he was willing to help us in any way that was within his power."

An emotional outburst by McKay during another phone call from M3 on Monday, 19th January, convinced Smith that the task of handling the phone conversations had to be removed from those members of the family whose feelings, understandably, ran away with them when in contact with the putative kidnappers. The police had coached them in what to say and do: let the caller do all the talking, keep the conversation going, and press him for proof that Muriel was still alive. Jennifer and Diane, like their father, were over-anxious and consequently tended to dominate the conversations. After the 19th January phone call Smith was able to come to an agreement with the family that they should leave the talking to Ian McKay.

In the opinion of the detectives Ian was the man who helped to weld the family together again after the early disagreements. Commander Guiver said of him: "Once he appeared on the scene we were able to take control of the family as well as the case. He decided the family had got to co-operate in every way with us. He was the one man who could draw out M3. He was someone I really respected, someone who would place his own instincts secondary to the police needs. As link man, he was able to draw M3 out, to get them to the point where they named a rendezvous. Mind you, it didn't happen straightaway: it took four or five calls to build up an understanding." Smith too thought that Ian McKay ("a most sensible young man") was the key to getting a rapport with the McKay clan. Smith came to rely a good deal on Ian, who had guessed early on that his mother must be dead.

The call Alick McKay had taken was a long one. M3 had immediately identified himself and demanded a first delivery of £500,000. McKay would get a letter from his wife and instructions about how to pay the money. Alick asked for proof that they had his wife: get her to tell them what Christmas presents she had had from her husband and children; what were the full Christian names of her children; get her to write out the page one headlines in the *Evening News* and send them to St. Mary House. None of this proof was ever forthcoming, needless to say.

McKay became visibly upset: "Bring a gun here and shoot me rather than make impossible demands ... nobody has got a million pounds and it is ridiculous to talk about it. You might as well give me ten years [to raise the money]. You might as well kill me now."

"If you don't co-operate. . ."

"I am co-operating but I can't co-operate with impossible demands ... make it a reasonable sum of money. I can kill myself. That would solve the problem ... have me instead. Take me instead. I can't give you what I haven't got."

"If you do not co-operate you will be responsible for not seeing your wife again."

"What have I done to deserve this?"

"I do not know. But your wife is a lovely person."

McKay offered £20,000 on the first delivery. M3 replied:

"That's not enough money in this country. That's not enough pounds. It's up to you to get the money. It's an order. It must be half-a-million, first delivery."

Alick McKay was utterly dejected after the call. There seemed no hope of making M3 see sense: although well off by most standards, McKay was far short of being a millionaire. Still, there had been the promise of another letter from his wife and, to McKay, while there was life there was hope.

The next day's mail was sorted and re-sorted for Mrs. McKay's letter. Further disappointment: nothing from her. Were they again the victim of a hoax? The following day, a Wednesday, there was still no sign of the letter. But in the morning there was a phone call from M3.

Ian took it and was told by the anonymous voice that two letters from Mrs. McKay should be at the house the following day. The caller said that before they could make a deal, however, the police had to leave the case.

Ian said, "We can't get rid of them ... they even suspect him [Alick] ... no, the phone isn't bugged as far as I know." (This with the tape-recorder softly whirring in the background.)

M3 said that in the letters Mrs. McKay had tried to indicate where she was being held "so we had to clip a few pieces out of it." Ian asked what proof the letters contained that his mother was alive. "When you read the letters you will see," he was told.

In a second call that day, M3 claimed that his code sign stood for Mafia gang three: he was the gang controller. He repeated the demand for one million pounds.

Two letters and a further ransom demand arrived at St. Mary House the following morning, Thursday, 22nd January. The apparent confusion over the arrival of the various letters from Mrs. McKay and M3 confirmed the police view that the missing woman had been made to write a series of letters in the early days of her confinement. It also seemed that M3 had slipped up by sending out the letters in the wrong order. Here were two arriving more than three weeks after the kidnapping which were obviously intended to have been sent out much earlier. One letter talked about seeing her daughter Diane on the television: those appearances had taken place on 31st

December and 1st January. Both letters also gave instructions
to deal with a gang giving the code M3: yet M3 had identified
himself over the phone long ago.

The letters and the ransom note all arrived inside an envelope postmarked Wood Green: 2:15 P.M.: 21.1.70. As in the
earlier letters, the script meandered from side to side without
any form of alignment: it was as if it had been written in the
dark.

The letter to Alick read:

> I am deteriorating in health and spirit... please co-
> operate... excuse writing I'm blindfolded and cold...
> Please keep the Police out of this and co-operate with the
> Gang giving Code No. M3 when telephoning to you.... The
> earlier you get the money the quicker I may come home or
> you will not see me again. Darling can you act quickly...
> please please keep Police out of this if you want to see me.
> Muriel.

There was another letter to Diane.

> Dearest Diane I heard you on T.V.... Thank you for look-
> ing after Daddy.... Would you please persuade Daddy to
> co-operate with M3 Gang... they will telephone you giving
> that code M3... M3... You will then be sure you are speak-
> ing to the right party.... Act quickly for my sake dear....
> Please keep Police out of it if you want to see me alive....
> Negotiate with Gang as quickly as possible and discretely
> [sic] for the gang is too large to fool.... All my love to
> you.... Mumm.

Then there was the ransom note:

> This is your instructions. Please pay: no error must hap-
> pen. You have no alternative. You will be advised not to in-
> form the police or any other party. If you disobey you will
> be to blame for the consequences. We are demanding one
> million pounds in two amounts. On the first occasion place
> half a million pounds in black suitcase in five and ten pound
> notes. You must drive your wife's Capri car unaccompanied
> from your home. Get onto the North Circular Road. Keep

driving until you approach the A10 Cambridge Road. As soon as you drive on the A10 road at the first set of traffic lights on the left hand side you will see a public telephone box at the junction of Church St. Enter the telephone box and wait for us to telephone you with further instructions at 10 P.M. on 1st February.

Your wife Muriel has pleaded with us that you cannot obtain one million pounds. If you send the first half million, the gang will hold a conference whether to accept the half million. If you agree you will receive your wife back in two days time.

Make sure the suitcase with the money is locked. We are sending a totally strange person who will be paid to do a job. His job will be to collect a black suitcase. If he is caught he will not be able to assist you or the police.

Any error on your part will only take two minutes and you will never see your wife. You will see her dead and delivered to your door.

Now certain they were dealing with Mrs. McKay's kidnappers, the police were gratified that the case was at last taking on a momentum. What was more, a geographic pattern was beginning to form, pointing to the north London area within the triangle created by the A10 and A11 roads and the northern outskirts of the capital. It remained to be seen whether this was all a decoy to draw them away from the real target.

Friday, 23rd January

Three more calls from M3 reached St. Mary House the next day. Even if the family had wanted to, it was difficult to stop the man from talking now that he seemed to have reached some understanding with Ian McKay. As Smith said, "He babbled on like Tennyson's brook." To Guiver "it seemed clear we weren't dealing with professionals. To them it was more a game of cowboys and indians."

The first call arrived at 10:37 A.M. "This is M3. Did you receive the letter?"

"Yes, we have, we received it yesterday . . . there's no proof in the letter that she is alive and well . . . this letter could have been written weeks ago. We have the money but why the hell should we give you the money unless we know she's alive?"

"I told you what she is wearing. What do you want me to do? Take her clothes off and send them in to you? We are in business and want to co-operate to sell good stuff. If you do not co-operate you will get her dead on your doorstep. I'm asking you for the last time, I'm asking you and that's if you intend to co-operate, yes or no."

"Of course we intend to co-operate. We want proof first. . . ."

"Well look you are not going to get—"

"Because you haven't got it! You've got a corpse, a corpse!"

"We've got her."

"You've got a dead person, you haven't got her at all. You know she's not alive so you are just trying to trick us. . . ."

"Look if you want to stick, we have got many jobs."

"How many kidnaps have you done then?"

"Never murdered anyone as yet, but there will always be a first time. You see now?"

"Okay then. But you get no money."

"I'm going to drop the phone on you."

Moments later, M3 was back on the phone, this time to give the family their "final chance" to co-operate. "Either you co-operate or we shall proceed. Then we will not be needing the money and you will not be seeing your mum again."

Ian asked for Mrs. McKay's voice to be taped or to let her talk to him but M3 refused. Then would he allow her to write another letter? No, they were not letting her write again.

The conversation ended with Ian storming down the phone, "Buy tonight's *Evening Standard* and get her to write out the headlines and the date in full."

"We don't have to co-operate with you. . . ."

"The headlines in tonight's paper and the date in full and I'm going to hang up on you. Goodbye!"

Ian's almost bullying attitude over the telephone, totally reversing the situation, only seemed to make M3 all the more willing to talk. Just after midday, he was on the phone again. He had just talked with Mrs. McKay, he told Ian. "Your mum says she has been a good wife to your dad and a good mother to her children. She asked why they had forsaken her? If you want your mum, follow instructions."

A weekend of enforced inactivity for the family was only

relieved on the Monday morning by the arrival of two more letters from Mrs. McKay. They were inside an envelope which contained yet another ransom note as well as three pieces of material cut from the clothes she had been wearing when she disappeared. These presumably were the letters that M3 had told Ian were on their way five days before. Again Smith's warning that before her death the gang got Muriel to write a series of notes to keep up the pretence of her existence over the weeks appeared to be coming true.

The two letters, both addressed to her husband, were again scrawled across single sheets of paper. The first, which began "Alick darling," was indecipherable in parts where words and sections of sentences had been written and then left tailing off in an ink splodge or a scratch of the pen. This letter read: "If I could only be home . . . I can't believe this thing happened to me . . . tonight . . . I thought of . . . see you . . . But it seems hopeless . . . that is all I can say at the moment. . . . You betrayed me by going to Police and not co-operating with the M3 Gang . . . Love Muriel."

In strict chronological terms that was probably the last letter Mrs. McKay wrote: the despair it expresses, the accusation of betrayal by going to the police, suggest she had then been in the hands of the Hoseins for some time. The second letter, like the first addressed to her husband, contained the same agonised cry for help and the same plea: "You don't seem to be helping me. Again I beg of you to co-operate with the M3 gang."

The ransom demand was written in bold, almost childish handwriting with many spelling and grammatical errors:

I am sending you final letter for your wife reprieve, she will be executed on the 2nd February, 1970 unless you keep our business date on the 1st of February without any error. We demand the full million pound in two occasion, when you deliver the first half million your wife life will be saved and I personally shall allow her to speak to you on telephone. We will not allow you to tell us how to run our organisation. We are telling you what to do. You cannot [the word "have" was crossed out and "eat" written above it] eat the cake and have it too. This is our 4th Blackmail, we have [the next word looked like "absorb," which may have been short for "absorbed"] 3½ million pound we did not murdered any one, because they were wise to pay up and their family were return to them, you do the same and she will return safely. My next Blackmail will be in Australia sometimes this year. Looking forward in settling our business on the 1st February at 10:00 P.M. as stated on last letter in a very discreet and honest way, and you and your children will be very happy to join Muriel McKay and our organisation also will be happy to continue our job elsewhere in Australia we shall look forward to see your son Ian when we visit Australia.

You see we dont make our customer happy we like to keep them in suspense in that way it is a gamble that is why we don't accept you Ian telling us what to do. We give the order and you *must* obey.

M.3.

Finally, the envelope contained three pieces of material, a small piece of green woolen cloth from the two-piece costume Mrs. McKay had been wearing, a snip of material from her black top coat, and a piece of leather cut from one of her shoes. As with all the other letters, these were scrutinised by the Yard laboratories. On the 4d. stamp, a left thumb print was found. It was not Mrs. McKay's: much later on it was found to be identical to Arthur Hosein's.

The kidnappers had chosen a Sunday for the payment of the money. The police spent the preceding days in preparation. Guiver and Smith attended a further conference at Scotland Yard with Peter Brodie to discuss the arrangements. Smith reported that Ian McKay had wanted to go on the money drop trip but had been successfully discouraged; it had been decided that Inspector Minors, posing as Ian, would go on the run instead. It was essential to have another policeman in the car too: the problem was how to persuade the kidnappers to allow two people to go along without frightening them off.

What if they kidded M3—providing he made contact again before the following Sunday, D-day—that the green Ford Capri had broken down? (One of the ransom calls had demanded that this was the car to be used.) Then they could send the Rolls instead and Minors' companion could act as chauffeur. Two alternative plans were hatched: if the Capri had to be used, one policeman would lie on the floor in the back of the car. If it was the Rolls, Minors himself would act as chauffeur and another man would dress up as Ian. Detective Sergeant Roger Street was chosen because he was of the same build and height as the younger McKay.

What about the money? Brodie asked. Guiver said he and Smith had already thought about this. They knew of a local printer in the Wimbledon area who could be trusted to do a secret job. Alick McKay was willing to loan them £300 in five pound notes, the serial numbers of which would be recorded. The printer would run off the remainder on paper which at first sight resembled real money, but only the edges of the paper could carry the engravings; the middle section would be blank. It would be quite impossible to use the money; but if it was prepared in bundles held together by a rubber band with the real notes on top, it would deceive anybody who flipped quickly through.

The danger was that other criminals might get to hear of the operation, and believing that £500,000 was in circulation, would attempt to hi-jack the suitcases. As Guiver commented later, "We could take no chances. If people of the same calibre as the Train Robbers had known all this money was on the move, they would have stopped at nothing."

Smith and Guiver asked Brodie for help, both with manpower and with guns. They felt both were necessary in order to mount guard over the money and to help with observation and protection while the ransom was being delivered. "It may sound fanciful, but we had no idea what we were walking into," Guiver said. "For the moment we had to accept that it might be the Mafia with all that that name meant." Brodie considered it an eminently reasonable request in the circumstances. He called in the then head of the Flying Squad, Commander Frank Davies, and Ian Forbes, in charge of the Regional Crime Squads, and explained the needs of the Wimbledon case to them. As a result, 180 policemen and fifty-six unmarked police cars were made available to Smith. In addition, the Criminal Intelligence Department at the Yard would supply men for the administrative side of the operation, both to try to anticipate the identities of the kidnappers from their own network of information and to spot any known criminals who might be caught in the police drag-net that was planned for the ransom rendezvous.

Both Minors and Street, as well as selected other officers, were to be armed. (The image of the unarmed British policeman is fast dying: in certain crimes of violence, notably bank and wage robberies, detectives are almost invariably armed during the search. In that same year, 1970, Scotland Yard was to send one of its leading firearms men to a three-week course at the FBI training academy in America to learn about training methods and new weaponry.)

Guiver was told that for the Sunday evening he would be able to use the main operations room at Scotland Yard in order to oversee the work. It had all the facilities necessary for such a complex job: telex machines, large-scale maps, open- and closed-circuit telephone. A reserve squad of detectives was to be held at Wimbledon in case the operation moved away from North London; other men were to be sent out early in the day to take up positions along the A10, while a third section, in cars and on motor-bikes, would follow the Rolls or the Ford on its journey.

Two questions remained to be decided. How were the police going to keep track of the money suitcase if by chance the kidnappers collected the ransom and got through the cordon? And how were the policemen in the car to keep in touch with their colleagues on watch in the area?

The answer to the first problem appeared to lie in experimental work done by the Home Office scientists on a homing device which enabled vehicles or objects to be followed by remote control. The device had first been demonstrated to the police a year previously at a Home Office exhibition at Coventry police training centre. Much of the work on it is still secret, but when it is refined plans are to use it mainly for vehicles carrying large sums of money or high-risk prisoners. An electronic "bug" attached to the object under scrutiny emits radio waves which are picked up at the monitoring station and its progress is charted on a map. Initially it had been found that as the bug moved away from the monitor its messages lost strength, and at any distance over five miles attempts to locate its position became very imprecise. Now, however, the Home Office has found a method of keeping the tracking line so precise that experiments have shown the bug can be tracked to within a few yards from fifty miles away.

Smith, who was to be in charge of operations out at the scene of the money drop, was to be given an unmarked police car and a driver. Over the police radio he could keep in touch with Guiver back at Scotland Yard but, more important still, the car was to act as the monitoring station for the bug which the Home Office scientists attached to the money suitcase. In this way, Smith would be able to follow the path of the suitcase wherever it was taken. The plan was not to pick up the kidnappers at the rendezvous spot but to follow them by means of the bug back to where they might still be holding Mrs. McKay. The police doubted that she was still alive, but they decided it was necessary to risk losing the criminals on the off-chance that they would lead them to the missing woman. Minors and Street were told that should they find themselves confronting the kidnappers and Mrs. McKay, they were to throw themselves on her to cover her body from any shots.

There remained the problem of keeping contact with the men inside the McKays' car. The scheme eventually agreed upon was hedged round with flaws. It was decided that Street should carry a two-way radio concealed in a sling in which his arm was to be bandaged. But first M3 had to be apprised of this idea and to approve it. *If* he rang between now and the money drop, *if* he sanctioned the use of the Rolls, *if* he allowed another person to come on the run and *if* he approved of the idea of "Ian McKay" (Street) having his arm in a sling, it might all work out.

But the days rolled by without any further contact from M3. The money had been printed, an outsize suitcase found to carry the bundles of notes, and the "fools' gold" placed under lock and key at Wimbledon police station with a full-time security watch on it. By Friday, 30th January, with only forty-eight hours to go, the police had almost given up the idea of using the Rolls.

But that day M3 rang. Ian had been schooled in what to say. "We're prepared to co-operate with you in every way we can."

"Okay, so it will be on the 1st, that's Sunday."

"Yes and I'll bring the money with me . . . look, I can't bring the Capri because the press are sitting outside . . . it's been in the garage for five weeks now and if it comes out they'll take pictures of it."

"Oh, I see."

"So I'll have to come in the Rolls. . . . I don't know the north of London very well and I've also injured my hand a bit and I want to bring the chauffeur."

"Oh, I see."

"Also if I take the Rolls out on my own they" [the waiting journalists] "have never seen me drive the Rolls before and they'll know what's going on."

"Yes."

As the phone was replaced on its cradle, there was a look of jubilation on the faces of the policemen at St. Mary House. M3 had swallowed the bait: it augured well for the Sunday.

Sunday, 1st February

For a day which held so much promise of an answer to the case—the capture of the kidnappers and the knowledge, one way or another, of Mrs. McKay's fate—this Sunday became something of a nightmare for the police investigators. When it was all over, they were scarcely any nearer to a result, and so much had gone wrong that there was an unofficial post mortem. Worst of all, there was the danger that they had frightened off the kidnappers. One senior policeman concerned with the operation later described it as a fiasco; Smith said that he nearly cried when he had to call off the job at three o'clock the following morning.

Everything went so wrong that it is astonishing the Hoseins were in custody within another six days. It certainly bore out Guiver's belief, with respect to the personalities of the criminals, that they were not dealing with professionals. An experienced criminal, aware as the Hoseins were after that disastrous Sunday that the police were all over the place, would have cut his losses and disappeared quietly. But the Hoseins were both foolish and greedy: they were like the monkey with its hand in the sweet jar. They would not let go.

On the Sunday afternoon, Minors and Street arrived at St.

Mary House to put on their disguises. Minors changed into a borrowed chauffeur's uniform while Ian McKay provided Street with one of his suits and the detective's hair was touched up at the edges.

During the day M3 phoned again to check that the deal was still on. He told Ian, "If everything goes smoothly you will see your mum tonight." He ordered that Mrs. McKay was not to be questioned by the police or by the press "on orders from our head office."

At nine o'clock that evening the Rolls swept out of the driveway with Minors at the wheel and Street sitting in splendid isolation in the back, his arm in a sling. They drove steadily through the empty streets of southwest London and picked up the North Circular Road, as instructed, soon after crossing the Thames. They reached the telephone box at the Cambridge Road-Church Street junction just after ten o'clock. Street went inside the box and the phone rang almost immediately. A voice said, "Who's that?" Street replied "Ian McKay; who's that?"

The caller said, "This is M3. These are your instructions. Proceed along the Cambridge Road away from London. At the second set of traffic lights on the left is Southbury Road, with a telephone box on the corner. The number is 01-363 1553X. Go there and wait for another call from me. Any error will be fatal."

Street got back into the car, told Minors what the instructions were, and, as the Rolls set off again, relayed the message into the two-way radio hidden on his arm. They drove to the second telephone box, arriving there about 10:45 P.M. The same method of contact was used; then M3 told Street to look on the floor where he would see a cigarette packet on which further instructions were written. Street stooped down and picked up the inside flap of an empty packet of Piccadilly cigarettes and saw a list of orders, signed M3.

He was to drive along the A10 to a village called High Cross where he would see a petrol station. Soon after that he would come to a road turning on the left to Dane End. There "McKay" would see two paper flowers on a bank at the roadside.

Street told M3 he had found the packet. The other man told him to leave the money by the flowers and then go back to the first kiosk at Church Street. "You will get a phone call saying where your mother is."

Until now the police had behaved with caution, not wishing to show their hand for fear of scaring off the kidnappers. Then, unaccountably, the operation took on a Keystone Cops flavour. Minors and Street were doing exactly what they had been told: driving to the Dane End junction to find the paper flowers on the bank. But both behind and in front of them policemen in the most unlikely of disguises had turned the A10 into a pantomime. Four police motor-cyclists, dressed up as Hell's Angels, were now tailing the Rolls. Although keeping their distance, they were sitting as erect in the saddle as if they had been on guard duty to the Royal Family. As one policeman said later, "They looked just like policemen in disguise." Further back along the road were convoys of plain cars manned by some of the 180 detectives concerned in the operation. One which contained four particularly villainous looking individuals was stopped by a local police patrol who thought they had stumbled on a London gang.

Minors and Street had arrived at the rendezvous at midnight. It had been arranged that Street should get out of the car and leave the suitcase, but at the last moment there was a hitch and both detectives carried the suitcase from the car to the side of the road. As they put the suitcase down, the detectives heard a rustling in the hedgerow. Minors told Street to walk slowly back to the car and lock himself in. Then as Minors was about to storm the hedge he saw a balding head peering at him through the branches. It was one of the police guard who had infiltrated the area. Minors' hand, which had flown instinctively to his gun, dropped to his side again and he walked back, heart thumping, to the Rolls, only to find he could not get in. Several moments passed before either man remembered that the doors were locked.

It was two very relieved men who finally headed the Rolls back towards London. They had carried out a difficult and dangerous mission: now it was for the back-up team to carry the operation through to fruition.

But the cars and motor-cycles which drove back and forth in front of the suitcase and the paper flowers had created something like a rush-hour traffic jam on this normally silent

Sunday night. And the police had not only overdone the car operation; they had flooded the ditches and fields surrounding the ransom spot with men crouching almost cheek by jowl with one another.

The suitcase remained at the roadside until 2.30 A.M. on Monday. In that time the numbers of all passing cars had been taken by the men sheltering in the vicinity. Detective Sergeant Arthur Stevens reported seeing a dark Volvo car with two people inside. He could not see the number but noted that one of the sidelights was not working. This description was passed on to the operations room at Scotland Yard where Guiver was coordinating matters with Commander Davies of the Flying Squad. In all the police logged less than a dozen cars in the area of the suitcase that night: the number of police vehicles outnumbered the ordinary traffic by almost five to one.

The dark Volvo 144 belonged to the Hoseins, and from the enormous activity around the ransom spot they were in no doubt, as they indicated later to Ian McKay on the phone, that the police were very much in evidence. The culminating blow to hopes of a capture came when the Hoseins, after driving past the suitcase, pulled into an all-night transport cafe a little way down the A10. While they were there, no doubt debating what to do next, a car pulled in and two men—obviously policemen although they were in civilian clothes—entered the cafe. Without any further ado, the Hoseins turned tail and headed for home.

Throughout the evening the police vehicles had kept in touch with each other, with Smith, and with the operations room at the Yard by radio. It was another error, though not one the Hoseins were able to exploit. The police have long known that their radio frequencies can be picked up by any outsider with a VHF wireless. The Home Office is experimenting with ways of overcoming this very grave drawback; in the meantime the police tend to use their normal frequencies only for routine messages. For secrecy's sake they often keep in contact with control by public telephone.

On this night, however, the police radios had been jammed with talk—comments like "Well, I'm here but I can't see anybody." One Fleet Street crime reporter recalls the phone call he got at about one o'clock on Monday morning. "It was from a man who makes a few pounds out of papers listening in to the police. He said: 'Hey, they're after John McVicar' (an escapee from Durham prison). In fact it was McKay, not McVicar. He had got the names mixed up."

Within twelve hours of the money being deposited by the roadside in rural Hertfordshire, the London *Evening News* was carrying a most detailed description of what had happened. It was acutely embarrassing for Scotland Yard, who feared that if the kidnappers read the story there would be no further hope of catching them. The Commissioner, Sir John Waldron, sent out a private and confidential notice via the Press Association to all editors asking them not to make any mention of the abortive ransom attempt, and *The Evening News* complied by dropping the story after the early editions. (Although the police can only ask, newspapers are prepared to respect such pleas unless it is obvious the force is covering up its own deficiencies.)

Some harsh words were later said by the various police contingents involved in the Dane End operation. One of the detectives gave it as his view that some detectives had gone on the mission in the belief that it was to be a "bash-grab" affair, when delicacy and secrecy were the necessary qualities.

The whole operation blown, Minors and Street were ordered to hurry back to St. Mary House as quickly as possible. Should M3 be so foolish as to ring again, Ian McKay had to be told what had gone on so that he at least could keep up the pretence of having been out at Dane End. The suitcase and the paper flowers were collected and taken away by the Flying Squad men. The flowers and the Piccadilly cigarette packet upon which M3 had written his instructions were later to help convict the Hoseins. Arthur Hosein's left thumb print was found on the cigarette packet and the flowers matched some found at Rooks Farm and in the Volvo a week later. To this extent, the day's work had not been a complete wash-out. But as an excuse to trap the kidnappers and find Mrs. McKay it had misfired completely.

Other Flying Squad officers were told to make enquiries in the neighbourhood to see if somebody who lived locally might have been connected with the crime. At this spot on the A10 there were only a few cottages. The lights in one of the houses had been on most of the night, and early Monday morning the detectives called at the local police station to find out who lived there. It turned out that there had been an illness in the house and the occupants were soon cleared of suspicion. Remembering the briefing they had received from Smith before starting out the previous night—"There are at least two, probably four, and we think they might be West Indians"—the Flying Squad men asked the station sergeant if he knew of any West Indians living in the vicinity. No, the sergeant replied. There were two coloured men living at a farm in a nearby village called Stocking Pelham but he thought they were Pakistanis.

On the Monday afternoon the detectives went to Stocking Pelham. Posing as insurance salesmen, they made enquiries amongst the regulars at the local public houses. It appeared the Hosein family was not particularly liked and were very much out of character in the rural English backwater. But of their criminal potential there was no evidence at all. The London detectives went back to their colleague at the police station. Yes, he had come across the Hosein brothers through various motoring offences. They had a Volvo car which was registered in Mrs. Else Hosein's name, as well as a Morris Minor. This incident, like so many others, was filed away in the unlikely event the Hoseins might crop up again.

A Volvo car had now entered the enquiry on three occasions: at Wimbledon on the afternoon of the abduction, at Dane End, and then in the ownership of the Hosein family. Should its significance have become apparent by now? Several thousand cars had come under police scrutiny in the weeks following 29th December. There were hundreds of Minis and Cortinas, but there were only three Volvos.

Monday, 2nd February

Minors and Street arrived back at Arthur Road in the Rolls before dawn, to be greeted by Smith. There was a mood of hopelessness in the house amongst police and family. Was it even possible that M3 would ring again if he knew the degree of police involvement in the trap? Smith could only hope that M3's absence from the rendezvous was because of some other reason and that perhaps he had not been aware the police were present.

But to be on the safe side Ian McKay was again coached about what he should say if a further call came. And, unbelievably, within a few hours M3 was on the line again. Smith's faint hope that the police had not been spotted was soon shattered. Angry at being tricked, M3 told Ian that he had not realised the Rolls was being tailed until he radioed "the Boys." M3 added, "The boss laughed and said he had seen cars around the pick-up spot. . . ."

M3 said he was now going to a midday meeting between the "semi-intellectuals"—the bosses of his organisation—to decide the time at which Mrs. McKay was to be executed. "I am going to plead for your mum to the semi-intellectuals. I am fond of her—your mum—you know. She reminds me of my mum."

Ian had tried manfully to get across the story that the police had been at Dane End without his knowledge. To some extent he appeared to succeed, but the understanding between him and M3 had now been eroded. M3 insisted that if he rang again he would talk only to Alick McKay.

As if Guiver and Smith and their teams were not already despondent at the Dane End debacle, a further piece of trouble awaited them at the Yard that day. Brodie rang to say that the Commissioner had received a phone call from the Chief Constable of Hertfordshire, Mr. R. N. Buxton, that Yard men and Metropolitan police officers had entered his territory the previous night without first seeking formal approval. A discreet word of explanation and apology soon set the matter aright. But as Guiver said later, "What were our men to do? Were they to get out of their cars the moment they put their feet into Hertfordshire territory and ring up the nearest police station? There was such a need for secrecy that even half of our men did not know the full story."

Contrary to their own wishes, the police were forced to bring Alick McKay back into the picture: he was now the only person with whom M3 was willing to talk business. What persuaded the kidnappers to persevere when even they must have sensed they were playing with fire nobody knows. Perhaps it was the way in which Ian McKay, in his last conversation with them, had told a sufficently tempting story about the half a million pounds (he said there was going to be trouble with the tax people over it) to lure them on to disaster.

But Smith was still adamant that if it ever came to another ransom money trip, McKay senior was not going. This time Inspector Minors would impersonate the head of the family so, when M3 rang twice on Thursday, 5th February, talking about further arrangements for the payment of the £500,000, Minors himself was listening in to the calls on the extension.

This time M3 wanted the money in two briefcases. McKay, guided by Smith, said the money would not fit into briefcases. Eventually they compromised on two suitcases. Alick was told that the next afternoon, a Friday, he and his daughter Diane were to take the Rolls and drive to the same telephone box in Church Street, off the Cambridge Road in North London. They were to get there at four P.M. and wait for further instructions.

This time there was less than twenty-four hours for the police to set up their counter-plans. Smith and Guiver immediately went to the Yard to see Brodie, Commander Davies, and Commander Forbes of the Regional Crime Squad. This time they agreed that after the Dane End experience there was to be complete radio silence and no overt attempt to track the Rolls. Except in an extreme emergency, all communication was to be made via the public telephone system.

The Home Office agreed once more to fix a bug to the suitcases and suggested the use of a helicopter to help track the Rolls if the car should be waylaid and it and its occupants taken away by the kidnapping gang. The Rolls was taken to a Home Office research establishment and a large white phosphorescent blob was painted on its roof to help the tracking helicopter. When the police at Wimbledon saw the white circle they almost collapsed with dismay. If the words "Kidnap Car" had been written on it in large letters the purpose of the Rolls could not have been more obvious. Rags were produced and the white mark polished out until it was little larger than a pigeon's droppings.

Not having their own helicopter, the police borrowed a machine through the good offices of the *News of the World*. Detective Sergeant Bill Jones was to act as observer to try to follow the McKay car if all other plans failed. As it turned out, the helicopter never left Elstree aerodrome in Hertfordshire where it was based awaiting instructions. Though the helicopter had special clearance to fly at night if necessary, the Rolls was never to figure in the second rendezvous attempt.

As the signs indicated that the A10 road would again figure in the plot, the head of Hertfordshire CID, Detective Chief Superintendent Ron Harvey, a one-time Scotland Yard man, was also brought into the operation. With his help the A10 and every road which linked it was to be covered by car teams from the Flying Squad and the Regional Crime Squad. As the kidnappers' trail appeared to be moving in a northerly direction away from London, the teams of detectives were placed along an arc spreading through Hertfordshire and Essex, bisecting the A1, A10 and A11 roads. From here it was hoped that they would move inwards, trapping the kidnappers in a pincer movement. To maintain contact with headquarters control, they were to use the landline system—public kiosks. Where possible they were virtually to take over a box and keep an open line to the Yard.

To avoid turning the final rendezvous into something akin to a policeman's ball, it was decided that this time only a select few detectives should be on hand ready to move in to the spot named by the kidnappers. Even this idea had its risks. The hazards of the operation were compounded by a proposal that a third man should be along in the Rolls, hidden from view, to go wherever the suitcases went. Success depended upon many contingencies, not the least of which was that at some stage the officer might find himself on his hands and knees in an open field with no cover in reach. It was a brave but rather desperate plan, which could place Mrs. McKay herself in jeopardy if she was still alive: if the kidnappers saw the policeman they would know the game was up and might turn on her.

Detective Sergeant John Bland of the Flying Squad, a man who knew how to look after himself in difficult situations, was chosen to ride in the boot of the Rolls. Ventilation was provided by removing a section of the rear seating upholstery.

Minors was sent home to shave off his moustache. Something fell from his pocket and his wife, picking it up, found it was a toy gun. As Minors recalled later, "What she didn't know was that I had a real gun already loaded deep in my trouser pocket. The toy was there to fool the kidnappers if they caught me and ordered me to throw my gun in."

Woman Detective-Constable Joyce Armitage, on loan from Scotland Yard, was to play Diane Dyer's part in the car. She is an attractive red-head who has worked on several undercover assignments for the police; her husband is also at Scotland Yard.

The sham McKays were kitted out in the house from Alick's and Diane's wardrobes. Bland climbed into the boot of the Rolls while it was still in the garage and at three o'clock on Friday afternoon, 5th February, the car set out, the same dummy money overlaid with real five pound notes in the boot with Bland.

4 P.M. Friday, 5th February until 3 A.M. Saturday, 6th February

Coincidental with the departure of the Rolls from St. Mary House, the Commissioner of Police put out a further directive to the press through the Press Association. Its aim was to silence any rumours about the night's operation. In spite of all the precautions the police had taken, there was still the chance that a newspaperman might get to hear of it.

The P.A. memorandum said:

Private and confidential memo to editors not for publication. We have been requested by Scotland Yard to circulate the following:

The Commissioner of Police, referring to reports that reached the Press of enquiries being made in the Ware, Hertfordshire, area* in connection with Mrs. McKay would be grateful if editors would refrain from any mention of this fact as publication would seriously interfere with police enquiries still continuing and might endanger Mrs. McKay's life. (See confidential guidance note.)

This request covers any further police activity of this type (repeat of this type). Editors can be assured that as soon as there is information available that does not jeopardise either of these considerations it will be made available to the press.

---

* A reference to the Dane End ransom drop operation.

Note for confidential guidance. Certain items of clothing belonging to Mrs. McKay have been received by the McKay family from the person or persons who are demanding a ransom for her release.

This information was given to the daily press last Monday for guidance only, not for publication, for the purpose of assuring them that the police have good reason for fearing Mrs. McKay's life might be endangered if police activities such as those at Ware were published.

The police were not being entirely frank: they were convinced Mrs. McKay was dead by now, but that was as yet an unsubstantiated view and one best kept from the ears of Fleet Street.

The Rolls arrived at the telephone box in Church Street, Edmonton, at 4 P.M. Minors went to the box and waited, but it was another forty-five minutes before the phone rang. The caller asked "Alick McKay" to identify himself. Satisfied with the answer, the caller announced that he was M3 and told Minors to go to another public call box, this time in Bethnal Green Road.

When Minors' instructions were relayed to Guiver, again in the operations room at Scotland Yard, there were some moments of despair among the backroom men. Minors now had to double back some five or six miles into the heart of London and away from the concentration of police support. Although men had been held in reserve at Wimbledon and at Scotland Yard for such a contingency, it was doubtful whether they could reach Bethnal Green, a working-class district on the fringes of the City of London and the East End, in time to get into position in case M3 made his strike there.

Guiver conceded later, "This was the one eventuality we hadn't counted upon." There was a short but concentrated debate in the operations room; finally Minors was ordered to keep to M3's orders and go to Bethnal Green Road. "But take it slowly so that we can get some men there first," he was told.

The Rolls arrived outside the Bethnal Green Road phone box at six o'clock. Fortunately for the police the kiosk was within a few yards of a police station: it made observation of the box and the street a comparatively easy task. (Even so, unknown to the police, Nizam and Arthur Hosein were sitting in a car parked in Bethnal Green Road scarcely two hundred yards from the phone box. The brothers waited until Minors pulled up outside the kiosk and then drove off to put through the call "Alick McKay" was waiting for.)

When that call came, Minors was told by M3 to leave the Rolls at Bethnal Green underground station and take the Central Line train to Epping. There he was to await a further call in the phone box by the booking hall. "No error must be made. If the police are around this time, we will execute Muriel and no one will ever see her again."

Then M3 asked to speak to Diane Dyer. Woman detective Joyce Armitage came to the phone and heard a voice say "Hello Diane. Have you got the money in the suitcases? You and your dad go to the nearest tube station, taking the suitcases with you.

"Take the tube down to Epping. This is your last chance, any error will be fatal to your mum. When you get to Epping, you will see a telephone box there. The number is 3077. You will be called there."

Armitage said she was upset and passed the phone back to Minors, who said into the mouthpiece, "We will do as you say."

The kidnappers had again switched the trail leading to the rendezvous in a manner which was quite disconcerting to the men trying to trap them. By that time of night the tube trains were full of commuters leaving the City and the West End for the week-end break. If the gang attempted to hi-jack the money on the train there might well be bloodshed on a large scale. To be safe, it was necessary to get detectives into every carriage: again this would take time to arrange. Cover would also be needed for the money and for those carrying it in the booking hall at Epping. It all depended on whether the Rolls was already under scrutiny. If it was not, then it might be possible for Minors and Armitage to go straight to Epping and cut out the potentially hazardous train journey.

This debate occupied those in the operations room for several minutes. In itself it gives an insight into the workings of the mind of the experienced detective. Here were men debating matters which could be of life-and-death importance both to Mrs. McKay and to the police officers in the Rolls. And a decision had got to be taken quickly. Again their yardstick was their knowledge of the criminal mind, how it would react to given circumstances.

While some of the operations team were in favour of the Rolls going straight to Epping, others thought it dangerous to disobey M3 and considered Minors and the others ought to get on the tube at Bethnal Green as ordered. Finally a compromise was reached: Minors was told to drive as far as Theydon Bois (the Central Line stop prior to Epping) and get on the train there. He was told to drive slowly to give the operations room time to get detectives, in various disguises, on to the train and more men to Epping station.

The manpower situation was getting difficult. Scotland Yard had already received a call from Essex police saying a householder living near North Weald airfield claimed to have spoken to Mrs. McKay herself! When questioned, the man said he had had an anonymous call telling him the police would find Mrs. McKay at the airfield—a war-time base now used only by flying clubs. The man further said that a woman had been put on the line representing herself as Mrs. McKay.

North Weald is only about three miles from Epping. The police had to consider whether it was a deliberate blind by the kidnappers to draw their forces away from the epicentre of the operation. They could not afford to overlook any possibility, however, and they recalled, without much enthusiasm, that the Dutch medium Croiset had mentioned "a deserted airstrip" in his original prediction, made as long ago as 1st January. The airfield was searched that night and again the next day without success.

It was dark by the time the Rolls inched into the car park attached to Theydon Bois station. In a remote corner of the park, the boot opened and a dishevelled Bland climbed out, clutching the suitcases. Minors and Joyce Armitage boarded the next train for the short trip to Epping. He advised her that if at any time they met the kidnappers face-to-face, she was to try to get into a ladies toilet and lock herself in: she was not to come out again until she heard his voice. Bland got into another carriage; in the various compartments were detectives disguised as office workers, labourers and railwaymen.

The six-minute journey from Theydon Bois to Epping

passed without trouble. Minors carried the suitcases into the main hallway of the station and stood outside the kiosk with Joyce Armitage. At 7:30 P.M., M3 rang: "Alick, are you there?"

"Who is that?"

"M3. I see you are being watched."

(Again it appeared that the police had been rumbled: possibly M3 had noticed them in the Bethnal Green Road near the phone box. Yet the kidnappers were still prepared to put their heads further into the noose they knew was waiting for them.)

Minors was told to take a taxi and go to Gates Used Car Salesroom at Bishop's Stortford, a market town and light engineering centre thirteen miles away. There he and "Diane Dyer" would see a mini-van, UMH 587F, parked on the forecourt. They were to place the suitcases by the van and then go back to Epping to await instructions about how they could locate Mrs. McKay.

"If you do not drop the money, she will be dead. You must trust M3. We deal with high-powered telescopic rifles. Anyone trying to interfere with the cases—we will let them have it." And M3 added that the warning went for the police too. Robert Kelly, a car-hire driver of Centre Avenue, Epping, got a radio call a few moments later to go to Epping underground station and pick up a Mr. McKay. Mr. Kelly collected a tall, smartly dressed man wearing a camel-haired coat and fur hat. He was accompanied by a woman and carried two white suitcases. They put the luggage in the boot of the Ford Zephyr hire car and set off towards Bishop's Stortford.

While waiting for the taxi, Minors had put through a call from the station phone box to the Yard operations room, giving directions about where they were headed. The men selected for the job of surrounding the ransom drop spot, armed as were Minors and Bland, moved into position around the used car lot to await the arrival of the taxi.

For the taxi driver, Mr. Kelly, the antics of his passengers in the next few minutes looked like a high farce: either that, or he had fallen among thieves. Two hundred yards down the road from the tube station, the male passenger ordered the taxi to stop. The back door of the car was flung open and a villainous-looking man emerged from the shadows, got in, and lay down on the floor in the back. Mr. Kelly, considerably alarmed, asked what was going on. "We're playing a joke on a friend," replied "Mr. McKay" who indicated that the car should proceed and that it would be better if Mr. Kelly asked no further questions.

As they drove along the A11 towards Bishop's Stortford, Kelly heard the man in the fur hat say to his colleague lying on the floor, "When we get there, John, you had better crawl out and get behind the hedge. You'll get a good view from there . . . the others will be waiting." As the taxi neared the town, Kelly was asked to stop again and wait while the suitcases were taken from the boot and placed on the floor in the back of the car, alongside the third passenger. Then he was ordered that on reaching Gates Garage he was to drive past, turn around and on the return circuit stop, pulling in as close to the hedge as possible.

When that had been done, "Mr. McKay" and the woman stepped out. Then, before Kelly's disbelieving eyes, the man on the floor crawled out and scrambled away on his hands and knees, disappearing into the hedge. Finally, the suitcases were removed from the car and placed alongside a beige mini-car standing at the front of the car yard.

"Mr. McKay" and the woman returned to Kelly's car, got in behind him, and told him to drive them back to Epping. At midnight, after Minors and Joyce Armitage had spent a long, fruitless vigil outside the phone box in the station waiting to hear from M3, they asked Kelly to take them on to Theydon Bois station where they picked up the Rolls again.

For his five hours' work, Mr. Kelley received a £5 fare and a small tip. Some weeks later he received a visit from the police: his passengers on that night, they explained, had been detectives on an extremely secret mission and they thanked him for his co-operation. As the taxi driver said later, "There were times when I thought of leaving the car and running for it . . . there was no logical explanation for what was going on. I didn't sleep properly for about three days puzzling over it, and I don't mind admitting I was frightened."

It may have seemed to Mr. Kelly rather like a badly scripted B movie, yet there are many occasions when police have to adopt unconventional poses to gain an arrest. The Regional Crime Squads are known—and disliked in some police circles —because of the lengths to which they go in getting their detectives to be as inconspicuous as possible: clergymen, pregnant women, courting couples, any disguise or ruse as long as it gets them close to the criminal.

There had been some debate between Minors and the Yard planners about the wisdom of taking a taxi out to Bishop's Stortford. It meant placing a civilian at risk when it was conceivable that M3, or a gang that knew about the money, would try to ambush the car on its way to the garage. But in the circumstances the policemen agreed that they had no alternative but to follow orders.

Bland had been in his make-shift hide-out opposite the garage forecourt for only about five minutes when he saw a blue Volvo, registration number XGO 994G, coming slowly along the road. The single occupant appeared to look closely at the suitcases before moving on. About half an hour later, the Volvo returned, coming in the opposite direction this time, away from Bishop's Stortford town centre. The driver turned the car round, appeared to be contemplating the suitcases, and then disappeared again back towards the town. An hour later Bland saw the Volvo for a third time. This time it had two people inside and crawled past the suitcases at little more than walking pace.

At eleven o'clock that night some other people began to show interest in the suitcases, but not the kind of interest the police wished to arouse. They were a well-meaning couple, Peter and Joan Abbott, of Southmill Road, Bishop's Stortford. Mr. Abbott had noticed the suitcases as he was driving past and thought they had probably fallen off the back of a car. A public-spirited citizen, he left his wife standing guard over the cases while he went off to tell the police. The police said they knew all about the suitcases and that Mr. Abbott would do them a favour by forgetting he had ever seen them.

The Volvo had already aroused suspicions elsewhere. Michael Byers, a forecourt attendant at Gates Garage, had seen the car several times during the evening before the garage closed at ten o'clock. At one time the Volvo had been parked on the edge of the forecourt for several minutes. Byers went across and

asked the occupant to move on. The man he was later to identify as Nizam Hosein was looking at something written on a
sheet of paper—probably the one, later found in the pocket
of his trousers, containing the number of the mini van.
At 11:40 P.M., when these unforeseen interruptions appeared
to have frightened off the kidnappers, Smith called the operation off. The suitcases were collected and the disconsolate officers, cold and dirty from their evening's work in freezing
temperatures, made their way back towards London.

They were not to know that a tenuous link to the Hoseins
had already been established. Guiver later recalled the scene
in the operations room at Scotland Yard that night: "Reports
were rolling in over the landline system from the Essex con-
tingent of car numbers seen in the vicinity of Gates Garage.
One man called in the number XGO 994G and Derek Dilley*
turned to me and said: 'Hey, that's the car our people turned
up last week at Stocking Pelham.' The number came up several times that night and it was obviously worth a try. We
knew the car was registered in the Hoseins' name but we
double-checked with the car registry all the same. We decided
to visit the farm early next morning."

In the meantime, it was necessary for Minors and Joyce
Armitage to double back to Wimbledon once more to tell the
McKays the story of the second rendezvous, in case there were
more calls from M3. When they got there, unaware of the clue
of the Volvo car, a feeling of deep gloom descended on St.
Mary House. Minors and the woman detective were very tired,
but more demoralising even than the fatigue was the bitter
disappointment at the sense of a second—and surely final—
failure.

For an hour they sat brooding and talking dispiritedly with
Ian Burgess and the younger McKays. Then in walked Smith,
smiling broadly. "Don't worry; we think we may be on to
them." His mischievous grin removed some of the ache the
night's events had left behind: even at three o'clock in the morning St. Mary House came to life again.

---

* Commander Dilley, head of the Criminal Intelligence Bureau.

5
FROM ROOKS FARM
TO THE OLD BAILEY

IN THE MIST and mud of an English February afternoon two contrasting groups of people glowered at each other across a ford on the outskirts of the village of Stocking Pelham. A procession of police cars on their way to answer a call for reserves at Rooks Farm had run into the waters which had risen and covered the narrow country lane. Their presence was being viewed with some resentment by the members of the Puckeridge Hunt, whose unrewarding day in the saddle was no better for the arrival of the men in blue. One of the huntsmen, Peter Hamilton, a London businessman, recalled, "We hadn't had a scent all day and had just picked one up when we got stuck in this bog. The next thing we knew, there was a load of police cars in among us. We had no idea then what they were doing there."

The Master of Fox Hounds, Captain Charles Barclay, squire of nearby Brent Pelham, rose up in his stirrups and bellowed at the policemen in a stentorian voice, "Get out of our way." Not at all abashed at this confrontation with the might of rural Hertfordshire, the policemen grinned back: "Work before play. Get out of *our* way."

The impasse resolved, the fifty huntsmen and their one hundred foot followers picked their way through the flood, casting curious glances at the convoy of police vehicles which was even then turning into Rooks Farm. Seated in the Barclay's mud-spattered Mercedes, Walter Annenberg, the millionaire American ambassador to Britain, met his wife's eyes and shrugged his shoulders. If policemen chose to charge round English country lanes on murky Saturday afternoons, it was not for an American to question their motives. The Annenbergs were week-end guests of the Barclays and had been following the hunt in the comfort of the MFH's car. Neither they nor the riders were to know at that moment that the brush with the police cars had some connection with the Muriel McKay case.

Much had happened in the few hours since Smith's ebullient 3 A.M. arrival at St. Mary House. The Chief Superintendent had quickly obtained a warrant authorising him to search Rooks Farm for Mrs. McKay's stolen jewellery and had phoned Hertfordshire police to arrange a meeting at the farm gates with Ronald Harvey, the local CID chief. So at eight o'clock on that Saturday morning, some twenty policemen arrived at Rooks Farm. Parked outside the farmhouse they saw a dark Volvo and a Morris Minor convertible. As Smith and Harvey went up to the front door, two Alsatians set up a loud barking and growling from an outhouse at the rear.

The door was opened by Else Hosein. Smith was explaining the reason for his visit—he was looking for some jewellery which had disappeared—when Arthur Hosein appeared at his wife's shoulder. He immediately invited the police into the house. Smith again introduced himself and Harvey and again explained his presence. Hosein told him, "I know nothing. I earn over £150 a week. I do not deal in stolen property. You can look where you like."

Else Hosein was less inclined to welcome the visit of the police at such an early hour, and for a very understandable reason. She had only just begun the weekly wash and a pipe on the Bendix washing machine had disconnected itself, flooding the kitchen and living-room carpets. When the police walked in the water was almost an inch deep and Mrs. Hosein felt some concern for the state of her carpets. (The carpets at the farm were later taken away for forensic examination. Minute scrapings of flesh were found on them but because of their water-logged state there was no way of identifying their source; they could have been bits from a chicken that had been killed.)

Accepting Arthur's invitation to "look where you like," Smith asked Harvey to call in some of his men and they began methodically to go through the house, room by room. But there was no sign of any jewellery, and a first, quick look into outhouses showed no signs of Mrs. McKay herself.

But while Smith was waiting downstaris in the lounge a

detective, accompanied by Mrs. Hosein, appeared from one of the children's bedrooms and showed Smith a batch of blue and yellow flower shapes cut out of paper. They were flimsy, childish decorations of no possible value, yet they gave the police hope for the first time that their presence at Rooks Farm was not entirely pointless, for they were identical to the bits of paper left on the roadside at Dane End. Later Nizam's girl-friend, Liley Mohammed, was to tell the detectives that she had made them for the entertainment of the Hosein children.

Detective Inspector John Bland, the man who had hidden in the boot of the Rolls and then in the hedge opposite Gates Garage the previous night, had gone upstairs to help the searchers. In a bedroom he saw the outline of a man in the mirror. Turning to face Nizam, Bland recognised him as the driver of the Volvo car which had been snooping around the ransom suitcases a few hours earlier. Bland told the young man to come downstairs with him: in Smith's presence he identified Nizam as the man behind the wheel of the Volvo.

Arthur Hosein had overheard the denunciation of Nizam to Superintendent Smith and soon it was to be his turn. Detective Sergeant John Quarry, who had also been outside Gates Garage the previous night, told Smith he recognised the elder brother as the passenger in the Volvo.

With these identifications, Smith felt justified in stepping up the pace of the search and sent for more men to make a more thorough investigation of the outside of the farm.

Meanwhile there was still a lot of evidence to be gathered inside. On top of a radiogram the police found a tin of Elastoplast similar to the sticking-plaster discovered in the McKay house on the night of 29th December. Due to an oversight by the searchers, the tin was left behind and not recovered from the farm until a fortnight later, but other articles were more carefully gathered in: an empty Piccadilly cigarette packet similar to the one containing the Dane End ransom instructions, and, from Nizam's bedroom, an exercise book with blue-lined writing paper. On this paper, at a later stage, the forensic scientists were to find impressions corresponding with words and marks on Mrs. McKay's letters to her family. In a pair of Nizam's trousers, the detectives found a piece of paper with the number of the Mini at Gates Garage.

In Arthur Hosein's workroom at the farm, a detective found two pairs of tailor's shears which he handed to Smith. From the kitchen, another searcher took a bill-hook. Arthur Hosein told Smith it was the only bill-hook they had on the farm. "I borrowed it from a farmer friend. I wanted to chop up a calf. It was Nizam who did the chopping."

Smith asked Nizam what he had done with the calf. "We fed it to the dogs."

"What happened to the bones and the head?"

"Last time we saw it, it was out with the rubbish."

Smith showed the elder brother a box of pills one of his men had found in a cupboard. Hosein said a girl friend had got them for him some time ago to cure a headache.

A detective handed the Chief Superintendent a double-barrelled shotgun, both barrels of which had been sawn off. The elder Hosein admitted the gun was his but declined to say where he had bought it. Smith asked who had sawn down the barrels and what they had used. Nizam said he had cut them down; Arthur had borrowed a hacksaw blade from a neigh-bouring farm just after Christmas. The farmer who had loaned the blade said that when he gave it to the Hoseins the edges were finely honed. When it was returned around Janu-ary 1st, it was completely blunt. Scotland Yard's ballistics de-partment examined the gun and found that while the sawn-off ends were clean, the gun itself had been fired. The Hoseins were never able to explain satisfactorily why it had been fired. A neighbour said she had heard the sound of a shot coming from Rooks Farm around New Year's Day; there was also the statement from one witness that he had seen a cartridge in Nizam's pocket. But this evidence was too insubstantial to be brought to court.

Finally, a detective who had been examining the cars brought in another paper flower which had fallen down be-tween the driving seat and the door of the Volvo. He said that a broken light on the car matched the description of the Volvo which had been seen on the night of the Dane End operation.

With all this evidence, Smith felt they now had enough to justify further questioning of the brothers. Arthur and Nizam were taken to separate cars and driven away to London. The elder Hosein, who was travelling with Smith, kept up a one-way conversation throughout the journey. He talked almost exclusively about himself, how highly regarded he was in the Stocking Pelham area and of his ambitions to be a local councillor. He confided to Smith that he came from a very wealthy family; his father was a holy man with great influence in high places.

The brothers were taken first to Wimbledon police station. Later that day they were transferred to Kingston-upon-Thames, headquarters of the division which embraces Wimbledon. There they were first finger-printed and then placed in separate rooms for interrogation.

"First catch your man, then nail him," runs the old police saying. The detection side of the case was almost at an end: now it moved to the confrontation between detective and suspect.

For the next three days and nights Smith was not able to go home until the Hoseins were charged. The interrogative part of an enquiry is often a mentally strenuous activity for a detective. Here, with two men of entirely opposite personalities, the challenge to Smith was one of adopting the right attitude: first to meet Arthur's extrovert boasting and then to cope with Nizam's extreme nervousness.

Twice in the early days of his confinement at Kingston, Nizam attempted to kill himself. First he opened a window in the interrogation room and tried to jump out; then, when he was placed in a station cell, he tried to bang his head against the wall. Because of his instability, Smith had Nizam watched day and night after that.

The police were still a long way at this point from providing evidence on which the Hoseins could be charged They may have rightly assumed that if they had the men responsible for the crime evidence would soon be forthcoming, either in the form of a confession or the discovery of Mrs. McKay's body at the farm. From start to finish, however, this was to be a case where the progression was never straightforward. Instead of working from either extreme of the crime—a confession or a body—the detectives had to try to fill in these gaps.

Good detective work is a matter of a partnership between

policeman and scientist. Where the detectives were unable to make positive deductions about the guilt or innocence of the Hoseins, the result of the finger-print tests was to corroborate their suspicions absolutely. On that first night at Kingston, the news came through that Arthur Hosein's prints matched those on the ransom notes, the envelopes, and the cigarette packet and that his palm-print fitted the one found on the *People* newspaper. Guiver said later, "When those prints matched we knew we were home. We were jubilant." Forty days of unrewarding, slogging work: then a moment of sheer delight. Little wonder some of the detectives found time for their own alcoholic celebration that night.

Arthur Hosein's demeanour throughout the interrogations mystified the police. He talked cogently, conceitedly—it was often difficult to stop him talking—and appeared entirely oblivious to his predicament. Yet he said not one word that incriminated him. Later he was privately described by a lawyer as "an aggressive psychopath" and his brother as an inadequate one.

As soon as Smith saw Arthur, the Trinidadian told him politely, "You have a very difficult case. I want to help you." Then, shifting the conversation completely, he added, "I know this is an important case."

Smith asked what he meant. "Well, it's worth a lot of money, isn't it? I mean the press. They would pay a hundred thousand pounds for the full story, wouldn't they?"

At his next interrogation, Arthur showed that his fertile brain had been dwelling on this point. He announced to Chief Superintendent Smith that when he was acquitted he was going to Paris to write the book of the McKay story and then turn it into a film.

"I'm going to get Richard Burton to play you, Mr. Smith. And for Inspector Minors, I'll cast Roger Moore. And I'll get Frank Sinatra to play the judge."

Smith, amused by all this, said, "Frank Sinatra! Oh, it's going to be a musical then?"

"No. Can't you see the connection? Sinatra—the kidnapping." (Apparently a reference to the kidnapping of Sinatra's son.)

"Who's going to play you, Arthur?"

"Now who do you think? Sammy Davis Junior, of course!"
Nizam, on the other hand, seemed afraid of saying anything.
Highly strung and apparently in fear of his brother, he appeared much more likely to crack up, and on several occasions was on the verge of doing so. When he was interrograted by Detective Sergeant Parker he said, "Oh my! What has Arthur done to me? I had a date with Susan, a girl from the Tesco sausage factory at Bishop's Stortford." (That was on the night of the abduction. Nizam was to admit that this was a trumped-up alibi after the police had spent many hours trying to find the mythical Susan.) Asked where he had been on 29th December, Nizam began trembling. "Where did Arthur say I was? I was with my brother Arthur." Parker asked him if he had been to Wimbledon that night (29th December). Nizam replied. "I want to die. Let me die." When Parker asked him what was troubling him, the younger Hosein got to his feet, threw his arms around the detective's shoulders and started crying. "Kill me," he sobbed. "What have I done? Arthur always gets me into trouble. Kill me now."

The legal advisers to Nizam found it difficult to communicate with him. For the first six weeks he refused to talk about anything to do with the case. Finally, Douglas Draycott, his Q.C., persuaded him at least to look at the statements which the prosecution witnesses had made.

The two brothers made an odd and contrasting pair. In one room sat Arthur, small, dark, and domineering, dictating statements by the ream to his solicitor's clerk and a typist. And in the next cubicle was Nizam, tall, ungainly, nervously silent.

The search of the farm at Stocking Pelham was to continue in fits and starts through the spring and summer of that year. On the first week-end, more than two hundred men went through the house and outbuildings and over the ten acres of land, most of it under ice and snow. One policeman was lowered down a 134-feet-deep well at the rear of the farm. The well, which had long been in disuse, had been covered in with wire and cement which had to be pulled and chipped away before the policeman could be winched down, carrying a powerful light rigged up from a portable generator brought in by the police teams. Mrs. Hosein, it was said, had given the police permission to do their searching and was supplying cups (or should it have been urns for two hundred thirsty men?) of tea. By now sinister rumours of the part the pigs at Rooks Farm might have played in Mrs. McKay's death had begun to circulate. Smith discovered that the Hoseins had kept seven Wessex Saddlebacks. By the time the police reached the farm four had been sold and only a boar and two sows remained. The pigs that had been sold were traced but by then they had been killed off. Thus it was never possible for the police to search the remains of the animals for cortizone, the drug which Mrs. McKay had been receiving, as suggested by scientists who thought that traces might remain in the bones of the beasts.

The police were still insisting on absolute secrecy about the search at Rooks Farm and the detention of the two men at Kingston police station. But it was impossible to keep anything from the ears of the newspapers in this case and all the Sunday papers were carrying stories that two brothers had been taken in for questioning about the disappearance of Mrs. McKay. The *Sunday Mirror* went one better and in an unrelated page one feature carried a large picture of Rooks Farm without naming it, merely mentioning that it was the scene that week-end of a large-scale police search. Once more the story drew the ire of Scotland Yard, on the grounds that it might prejudice enquiries that were still continuing. Again the Commissioner's directive went out to editors and, after the first editions, out came the *Sunday Mirror* scoop. Hindsight showed that the picture could in no way have embarrassed the police work, but in fairness to Scotland Yard it must be said that they use this power of "censorship by request" very sparingly. Only in the McKay case were they to wield the gloved fist with such regularity.

The questioning of the Hoseins continued over the weekend. They had been given proper access to their lawyers and the police were in no breach of their powers in keeping the brothers at Kingston. But the time would be approaching on Monday or Tuesday when Smith would have to decide whether to charge them or let them go.

English law is imprecise on the issue of how long a man can be kept without being charged. On the Continent there is a specific time limit of forty-eight or seventy-two hours in most countries; in America, except in extreme circumstances, more than eight hours would be regarded as intolerable. But English law lays down only that a man's voluntary detention in a police station before he is charged should be of a "reasonable period of time." In any case, any citizen with knowledge of a crime has a duty to help the police. Theoretically, as long as the Hoseins were only helping the police, they could have walked out of the police station at any time. But in practice this is not lightly done. Here the police had three, or at the very outside four days in which to assemble a case on which to base charges.

There was still every hope that Nizam might break down under questioning. At one moment, when he was shown the pieces of material which had been cut from Mrs. McKay's clothing and sent to the family, he appeared to be on the verge of a confession, but at the last second recovered his composure.

While the third day of the search at Stocking Pelham extended to twenty-five acres of fields and woodlands surrounding the farmhouse, the papers were carrying detailed stories of how the kidnappers (no names were printed at this stage: the outside world still had no idea it was the Hoseins who were being held) had planned to take Mrs. Anna Murdoch and had abducted Mrs. McKay by mistake. The stories even described the two trips with forged money made by the police disguised as the McKay family—right down to the clue of the paper flowers. The detail in the newspaper stories was astonishingly accurate. Once again, Scotland Yard was faced with a leak of huge proportions: such premature publication of evidence at this stage, it might be argued, would prejudice any potential juror who read the accounts. But if the source of the disclosures was ever traced, the police were not revealing it.

On Tuesday evening, 10th February, when time was beginning to run out, Smith decided he had sufficient evidence. The Hosein brothers were taken back to Wimbledon police station to be charged by the senior station officer, Chief Inspector Stevens. Later that evening the Police Commissioner, Sir John Waldron, paid what was described as a "duty visit" to Wimbledon. He had gone there to discuss the case with Smith and Guiver and to be told the basis on which the charges had been preferred, as well as the outcome of the search at Stocking Pelham. Now it was for the courts to take over.

On the same night that the Hoseins were charged, Scotland Yard appealed to members of the public to contact them if they "knew of men of Indian extraction who had offered jewellery for sale in public houses and other places." The jewellery of course was Mrs. McKay's: the police still had a vague hope that the brothers had sold the valuables to raise some spare cash.

After the first formal court appearance and remand at Wimbledon on 11th February, the Hoseins were to disappear from the public's mind for seven months, the time it took to prepare for their trial at the Old Bailey. That seven months constituted something of a record for the snail's pace of British justice. The delay was almost entirely the responsibility of the prosecution, the Crown legal department being reluctant to go to court on a murder charge without a body. The police were under some pressure in the intervening time to produce either the corpse or some evidence that could be put to a jury to explain Mrs. McKay's total disappearance.

When Rupert Murdoch and his wife Anna arrived back from Australia in early February, the Hoseins were already in custody. By sheer chance Murdoch's return to London was to give the police one of the many bits of evidence with which they were able to build up a strong circumstantial case against the brothers.

Murdoch, who knew much of the background of the McKay story already, was advised that in view of all the publicity given to his company Rolls, ULO 18F, it would be better if the number was changed. When Murdoch's chauffeur went to County Hall, Westminster, to fill in the necessary papers, the clerk said there was a note on the file that a Sharif Mustapha had been enquiring about the address of the owner of the Rolls. Mustapha had said his car had been in an accident with it. The chauffeur reported this to Murdoch, who contacted Smith at Wimbledon. When the police checked the address on the GLC motor registry file, they went to interview the real Sharif Mustapha. He had no knowledge of the incident, but he was a cousin of one Nizam Hosein.

Alick McKay returned to work on Monday, 23rd February. His colleagues were amazed to see him back behind his desk. One *News of the World* executive said, "We were all astonished here in Bouverie Street at the way Alick picked himself up off the floor after this terrible experience. I honestly thought we would never see him back in harness again. But after a few weeks, there he was in his office again and what's more he seemed to have got over it all."

Although the Hoseins were now in jail, the police enquiry continued on two fronts. One group was still at, or in the vicinity of, Stocking Pelham; the other at Wimbledon or Kingston. The police diggers moved on to land at Hall Farm, which skirts Rooks Farm. Later they shifted their activities to the village of Sleepy Hollow, across the county border in Essex. But whatever secrets the soil possessed, it kept.

At one moment it appeared that the forensic scientists had achieved the breakthrough Smith and his team had long been hoping for. One of Nizam's suits taken from his wardrobe along with other clothing, including shoes, boots and hats, was found to have no less than twenty-two fibres which matched the material from Mrs. McKay's coat. For a few seconds Smith believed he had the answer to his troubles; then he was told that the fibres could have come from any one of a hundred thousand similar coats. Like so much of the evidence, it was far too circumstantial to present in a court of law. Suspicion, yes; proof, no. The discovery was filed away and never again referred to.

The Hoseins, meanwhile, were being given various tests. Arthur readily agreed to put an example of his voice on tape so that police could compare it with the M3 recordings. But Nizam refused, as was his right. Both men were asked, and agreed, to give samples of their handwriting. The aim was to establish whether either, or both, of them had written the various ransom notes and the instructions on the cigarette packet. From the handwriting done by Arthur at the dictation of the police, Scotland Yard handwriting experts were able to say that he had in all probability written two of the ransom notes and the instructions on the packet. But there was nothing to match with Nizam's writing, apart from the number of the

Mini car at Gates Garage, scrawled on the piece of paper found in his trouser pockets at the farm.

The police were also now able to piece together minor points which, while insignificant in isolation, were capable of helping the case against the Hoseins. They found, for instance, that the brothers took the *People* newspaper each Sunday. It was a copy of the *People* which had been found at the McKay house with Arthur's palm-print on it and which could have been used to wrap around the bill-hook before its use at St. Mary House.

Then, through the index of statements built up by Parker, the detectives turned up the evidence of the Wimbledon motorist who had twice seen the Volvo on the afternoon of the abduction. The motorist had been circumspect in his description of the Volvo's occupants, but his evidence was still worth putting to a jury.

The Hoseins were being held on remand in separate cells in the hospital wing of Brixton prison (prisoners on remand on serious crimes are normally kept for observation purposes in prison hospital wings). On 13th March, Adam Hosein, a stockbroker living at Thornton Heath, Surrey, visited his brother Nizam. A prison officer sitting behind Nizam saw him walk over to the glass window partition which separates prisoners from their visitors and press a piece of paper against the window. The paper, which was later taken from Nizam, read, "Do not say anything to no-one, not even solicitor, that I was by you on Monday night [29th December]. Two farmers are saying that Arthur was down there by them that day and at 6:30 P.M. I was home."

The police were already well aware of the existence of the Hoseins' brother Adam. His flat at Thornton Heath was only about five miles from Arthur Road, and the investigators had to consider the possibility that Mrs. McKay had been taken there. They searched the flat but found nothing and were soon satisfied that Adam was not connected with the crime. But they knew that on the night of the kidnapping, Nizam had called at Adam's house to repay an old £3.50 debt which he peeled from a roll of notes. This in itself was unusual because Nizam had not seen Adam for some time and he rarely had any money of his own. On the same night Nizam had also called upon his cousin, Sharif, who lived at Norbury—again in the Wimbledon area. A reconstruction of the Hoseins' movements that night suggested that at least one of them had gone to St. Mary House, removed Mrs. McKay, bound and gagged, in the boot of the Volvo, and left Arthur Road at around seven in the evening. Then the Volvo had been driven back to Rooks Farm —a journey through heavy evening traffic which would take them two hours. That placed the return of the car and its "prize" to Stocking Pelham at about nine o'clock.

Though there was no proof—in fact the evidence from the Wimbledon motorist of two people in the Volvo suggested the contrary—some of the enquiry team wondered whether Arthur had not made the journey to Arthur Road, leaving Nizam back at the farm to provide an alibi for their movements. If the Wimbledon motorist was to be believed this would imply a third kidnapper in the gang. It was a theory upon which the police still keep an open mind, having no tangible proof to support it.

Later that evening, Nizam had certainly turned up both at Adam's and at Sharif's homes. (There was no further evidence of Arthur's movements that night: was he guarding Mrs. McKay and getting her to write the ransom letters?) Then Nizam faced the drive back to Stocking Pelham again and, on the way, the first telephone call at 1:15 A.M. to the McKay house. (Of all the phone calls made by M3, Nizam is considered to have made at least 80 per cent.)

On the occasion of the Hoseins' seventh court remand at the end of March, criticism erupted from the defence benches over the amount of time the prosecution was taking to prepare the case. Mr. Leonard Woodley, appearing for Nizam, said he might at some stage have to apply for a writ of habeas corpus. Arthur's counsel, Mr. Herbert Dunn, Q.C., told the magistrates, "On a murder charge the defence has a basic right in justice to know at a reasonably early stage what is the nature of the charge and the allegations against him."

The protests were made more as a matter of form than in any expectation of shaking up the processes of the law. The committal proceedings eventually began eighteen weeks after the brothers' arrest: their seventeen remands must be something of a record for the Wimbledon Magistrates Bench. But the magistrates were really in the hands of the prosecution lawyers, whose word is virtually a law within the law. Nothing that the evidence at the trial later disclosed ever justified such a delay. There could be only one explanation: the Director of Public Prosecutions was still chary about pressing a murder charge when there was not a scrap of evidence that the brothers were the killers—that is apart from the "irresistible inference" to which the jury came, that if the Hoseins kidnapped Mrs. McKay, they must also have been responsible for her death.

It was three months before Nizam's legal advisers were able to discover the reason for their client's continuing silence. Then it became apparent that even in prison he had been under immense pressure from Arthur. There had been the occasion when Nizam was beaten up by his elder brother during exercise; from that time on strict instructions were issued to the prison authorities to keep the two men apart.

Arthur had also been getting messages through to his brother telling him exactly what to say and what to keep quiet about. Nizam had been told that he was to go along with a story Arthur had concocted for his defence concerning the controversial Labour M.P., Robert Maxwell. Although the story was simple, as all good defences should be, it was so crude and untenable that it only served to decrease the elder brother's chances when eventually he told it to a judge and jury. Arthur's story was that one night he came downstairs at Rooks Farm to find four people, one of them Maxwell, talking to Nizam. They were forcing him to kidnap Mrs. Murdoch for them. The motive fabricated in Arthur's mind was apparently revenge: in his deviousness he hoped to imply that Maxwell, having been beaten by Rupert Murdoch in his bid for the *News of the World* empire, wanted to get his own back in this manner.

Under the stress of Arthur's repeated efforts to get him to agree to this tale, Nizam took refuge in silence. Eventually, however, he began to discuss the case with his legal advisers. They formed the impression that this quiet young man, scarcely more than a youth, was very much under the dominance of his brother.

The proceedings to have the Hoseins sent for trial began in June, by which time the mention of the name McKay had lost something of its sense of horror. Under a recently passed law, the proceedings were unreportable because the defence had not waived its right to secrecy. The one advantage the magistrates' court hearings had over the Old Bailey trial was that they heard the tape-recordings of the M3 telephone calls. The kidnappers' seventeen recorded conversations with the McKay family came over clearly. It was apparent to those who had heard Nizam speak that his was the artificially deep voice which had made most of the calls.

On the eve of the committal proceedings, Nizam asked to be allowed to see the detectives in the case. He was brought to Wimbledon police station to meet Smith and Minors. As before, the younger Hosein appeared to be on the brink of revealing some deep secret; but something continued to hold him back. Several times during the interview Nizam broke down, once to such a degree that the policemen fetched a doctor. But at the end of the interrogation the detectives were no nearer the root of Nizam's emotional upsets.

The brothers were formally committed for trial and then returned to their cells at Brixton prison. The week after the end of the lower court proceedings Nizam was yet again interviewed, in the presence of his lawyers, at Wimbledon. Chief Superintendent Smith produced the items of labelled evidence which had already been before the court. Their effect on Nizam was startling. At the sight of the bits of clothing said to have been cut from Mrs. McKay's coat, dress and shoes, he closed his eyes and started moaning, "Let me die, let me die." The bill-hook produced the same reaction: he started trembling and closed his eyes as though to shut the weapon from his mind.

By July, the police search had begun again, this time in Essex: first in Epping Forest, then at an abandoned farm just across the county border from Stocking Pelham, and finally in fields surrounding the neighbouring hamlet of Brent Pelham. The sole reward for this effort was one fox's skeleton. In August, the search moved back to the place the police were—and still are—convinced holds the secret: Rooks Farm. The outside was again thoroughly inspected. Ponds were drained, hedges and ditches dug over and fields once again scoured by lines of policemen moving like locusts over the weed-riddled land. An architect and builder who knew the farmhouse and had carried out conversions prior to the Hoseins' occupation was asked in by the police on a consultancy basis. His job was to discover whether anything had been done to the premises by way of hidden rooms or false walls where Mrs. McKay could have been hidden. His report was completely negative.

Then all the fire grates were dismantled. The makers of the kitchen fire which connected to the oven were asked down from Liverpool. They took the flue apart and in one of the bends found several deposits of calcium carbonate which appeared to be the remains of small bones; but they could have been the remnants of chickens thrown onto the fire.

Smith recalled the curious story that a woman living in the Stocking Pelham district had told him soon after the story of the Hoseins' arrest had appeared in the papers. She lived about one and a half miles from the farm and owned a Leopard dog, a rare breed used mainly in Texas for cattle minding. Around 1st January, this dog, which has an acute sense of smell, set up a shrill howling on the lawn of its home. When its owner came out to see what the trouble was she had smelt something in the air coming from the direction of Rooks Farm. She told the Chief Superintendent that the last time she had noticed such a smell it was coming from a crematorium.

If, without the benefit of inside knowledge, anybody could have satisfactorily explained Mrs. McKay's disappearance, it should have been these policemen and their colleagues the forensic scientists. The time and money invested in this part of the investigation alone would have paid for many a complete enquiry in a murder case. Yet on 14th September, 1970, when the Hoseins' trial opened at the Old Bailey, there was still not a shred of evidence to point to Mrs. McKay's whereabouts, dead or alive. It was as if she had walked off the face of the earth eight months before.

The trial itself was a curiously unsatisfactory climax—or anti-climax. It answered none of the questions (how? when? where?) that everyone was asking about Mrs. McKay. There was none of the thundering advocacy that one associates—but rarely gets—with a major case at the Old Bailey. The trial was clinically efficient but totally lacking in the sense of adding a dimension to witnesses and defendants: instead of bringing them to life, they appeared as cardboard caricatures.

Just one phrase by the Attorney General, Sir Peter Rawlinson, taking his first case since appointment to office by the new Tory administration, remains in the mind. Speaking of the Hoseins in their Volvo passing and re-passing the money suitcases outside Gates Garage, he likened them to "a crow around its meat." The phrase seemed to sum up the brothers' whole mentality.

Up to the very last moment, there was some doubt in the minds of those who had heard the committal proceedings that the jury would accept the murder charges where there was no evidence a murder had taken place. It may be that in choosing to turn on each other, instead of presenting a united defence, the Hoseins were their own jailors in the end. The Attorney General had scarcely finished his opening address to the jury when Nizam, through his counsel, Douglas Draycott, Q.C., was making seven damning admissions which were to tie him irrevocably to the crimes. Arthur, who was content to let the prosecution earn its money, was really condemned by the scientific evidence. Could he explain the eight prints left by him on various bits of evidence, the *People* newspaper, the letters, the cigarette packet? No, he could not: like the legions of criminals who had preceded him in that dock, Arthur Hosein had been trapped by a scientific "law" from which no accused has ever found an escape route: that there is only one owner of any given finger-print. We tend to take the evidence of finger-prints for granted, to be surprised if they are not there. That perhaps is the measure of their power.

On the last day of the trial, Tuesday, 6th October, 1970, the case had drawn together like a magnet the innocent characters in the piece from either end of the earth. There was Alick McKay, who had attended court every day despite the advice of the police to lessen his suffering by staying away; there was Ian McKay, newly returned from Australia, and his sisters Diane and Jennifer. And a few yards away sat Mrs. Else Hosein and her father-in-law Mr. Shaffie Hosein, respected elder citizen of Dow Village, California, Trinidad, who had travelled to London to be near the sons he no longer understood.

Arthur, in true egotistic vein, had decked himself out for this special day in a finely cut dark blue evening dress jacket and matching trousers. Arthur's sartorial habits had caused some trouble during the trial. The police had allowed his own tailor from the East End to visit him in prison, bringing several rolls of cloth which he displayed in the cell; Arthur eventually chose the dark blue. His wife asked him if she should pay the tailor in cash or with a cheque. Arthur replied, "Don't pay him now. I'll settle the bill when I'm acquitted. I always say a friend in need is a friend indeed." The bill came to fifty-four guineas. When on the final morning the suit had not turned up, Arthur threw a tantrum and refused to go into court. Peace was finally achieved with the arrival of jacket and trousers; Arthur went into the dock looking as if he were en route to the Guildhall.

But the venom of Arthur Hosein, which was so close to the surface throughout the proceedings, was to show through in these final moments. When the jury returned verdicts of guilty against both men, with a recommendation for leniency for Nizam, the brothers were given the right of the last word to the judge before sentence was passed. Arthur, ignoring his counsel, Mr. Barry Hudson, Q.C., launched into a diatribe against Mr. Justice Sebag Shaw, the presiding judge: "Injustice has not only been done, it has also been seen and heard by the gallery to have been done. They have seen the provocation of your lordship and they have seen your immense partiality. From the moment I stood in that witness box and named Robert Maxwell, I realised you were a Jew. Thank you, members of the jury: it was a grave injustice."

Nizam, advised by his counsel, wisely said nothing. It only remained for the judge to dot the i's and cross the t's: life imprisonment for murder, twenty-five years for Arthur and fifteen for Nizam on the remaining charges. The kidnapping and confinement of Mrs. McKay, said the judge, was cold-blooded and abominable. "So long as she remained alive [she] was reduced to terrifying despair in a way which has shocked and revolted every right-minded person."

The following morning the *Sun* carried a statement from

Alick McKay which best expresses the suffering he and his family had borne throughout this nightmare:

One can accept death in the ordinary way. It is something which has to be faced and one has to adjust one's life to take account of it.

But in these circumstances one is unable to accept the explanation of death without finding a body, although I am convinced Muriel is never coming home again. I must face this situation of course and face my life as best I can.

I suppose I do not want to know the brutal facts really, and yet I must always ask, how did she die, what happened to her, where is her body?

However much I try to escape the tragedy and hurt of it, I suppose I really would like to know the answers.

My family try to help me not to think about it. They are extremely good to me and I am never left alone for long.

6
MURDER WITHOUT A BODY

"DEAD MEN TELL no tales." But they do, of course. They have a nasty habit of telling the truth to policemen and pathologists, to the acute embarrassment of the man who wants to commit the perfect murder. But bodies can be disposed of without trace if they are placed in the hands of a professional "liquidator." In the aftermath of its clean-up of London gangs during the 1960s, Scotland Yard came to know of at least five men who had disappeared in ugly circumstances. They had been the victims of internecine criminal warfare and they had simply been erased by men whose job it was to make sure they never returned either horizontally or vertically. (Britain has seen the spectre of the liquidator comparatively recently: the American gangs and the Italian Mafia have long employed his services.)

Why then the surprise, and the three questions that are constantly asked in the case of Mrs. Muriel McKay: How was she killed? Where was she killed? What happened to her body? For her killers were neither professionals nor had the advantage of the help of "disposal" experts.

But, it is asked, Arthur Hosein had lived in the East End of London for several years; might he have come into contact with the kind of men who would do the job for him at a price? Is it not possible he hired one of them? The theory cannot be entirely excluded. But it is extremely unlikely in view of the fact that when Scotland Yard's criminal intelligence bureau (a listening-post and clearing-house for criminal gossip) took soundings of the underworld in the early days of the case to discover who was behind Mrs. McKay's kidnapping, there was not a single positive response. Nobody significant in the world of crime had the slightest idea who was responsible for Muriel McKay's abduction.

141

Of course, the demand for one million pounds for Mrs. McKay's return made everybody think of the great train robbers. But they were all behind bars, and men of their criminal calibre could be counted on a couple of three-fingered hands. It was the strange mixture of professional ruthlessness and amateur bumbling exhibited by the Hoseins that badly misled the police in the early days of the investigation. The skill of the abduction contrasted so markedly with the stupidity later shown by the brothers that many people concerned with the case have asked if there was not a "third man" whose part ended abruptly with Mrs. McKay's murder.

Scotland Yard detectives have retained an open mind on this issue. While they have no concrete evidence that there were three kidnappers/murderers, there are suspicions. Two inexplicable features in the case leave a question mark even to-day. One is the utter failure to find Mrs. McKay, alive or dead, and the other is the abrupt change in the kidnappers' behaviour from audacity to naivety. On balance the police think Mrs. McKay was taken to Rooks Farm, but they concede there is a volume of circumstantial evidence which points to her not having gone there. In those circumstances they were forced to look for other hiding places. Was it possible that the "third man" had hidden her, either where he lived or at some place he and the brothers had hired for the purpose? That someone else was Mrs. McKay's "keeper" is suggested by the fact that Arthur and Nizam Hosein were moving about Rooks Farm quite openly, and receiving visitors, during the days following the kidnapping. Would they have dared to do that if she was being held prisoner there?

It is well known that the Hoseins set out to catch Mrs. Anna Murdoch, wife of Rupert Murdoch, the Fleet Street newspaper mogul. Instead they blundered and got Mrs. McKay, wife of Alick, Murdoch's number two on the *News of the World*. The police have since asked themselves whether it is possible that the man who had master-minded the crime was so furious at the mistake that after Mrs. McKay was murdered, he refused to have anything more to do with the attempts to raise the one million pounds and left her body to the tender mercies of the Hosein brothers. His disappearance from the affair might explain the sudden change in the kidnappers' behavior. The kidnapping itself was carried out with skill and aplomb, even allowing for the fact that they had got the wrong woman. Men of the description of the Hoseins are a rare sight in the area of Arthur Road, Wimbledon, the householders are people of means, aware of the prevalence of burglaries in the neighbourhood and consequently on the lookout for anybody acting suspiciously. Nevertheless Mrs. McKay was taken without any alarm being raised.

It must be accepted too that she was disposed of with skill: yet from that moment on the actions of the Hoseins verged on lunacy. The two parts of the operation—the taking away of Mrs. McKay and then the demands for and attempts to receive the money—were so diametrically different in character that the police have since questioned whether this discrepancy could only be explained by the third man stepping out of the crime. If this was the case, it might be argued that the Hoseins, particularly Arthur, would have given him away to the police. But if he was a man who had exerted an evil influence this might account for their silence.

Were the kidnappers killers by intent when they set out to drive to St. Mary House on Monday afternoon, 29th December? Were they kidnappers who turned killers in cold anger when they found they had the wrong victim? Or did they suddenly find their victim dead on their hands? A positive answer to one of these questions would go a long way to solving the rest of the riddle. At the trial, the prosecution claimed that the murder was premeditated, that Mrs. McKay "had her death warrant signed" the moment the Hoseins burst into her living-room and that they had no intention of exchanging her for the one million pounds they were demanding in ransom money. There was the evidence of the ransom letters that the brothers had forced Mrs. McKay to write in the first two or three days of her captivity and there was the certainty, the Attorney General maintained, of her being able to identify them if she was ever turned free.

Mrs. McKay wrote at least five letters at the brothers' dictation to her husband and children. They were to be used later to give the impression that she was still alive. This alone suggests that the kidnappers must have known the letter writer would not be with them for long, and in the view of the detectives involved with the case, it is a strong argument for premeditation of some sort.

The issue of identification of the kidnappers is less conclusive. In many recent kidnappings abroad where the victim has been turned loose after a long period of captivity—mainly crimes with a political background—the kidnappers have worn masks and have never been seen by the victim. It was certainly not beyond the power of one or two strong men (masked when they entered the house?) to make sure Mrs. McKay did not see their faces.

But common sense suggests that it is doubtful whether the Hoseins intended to murder their victim from the very start of the plot. They were after money, and however limited their criminal psyche, it must have told them that dead people can exert no bargaining power.

If one excludes the idea of murderous intent from the very time the Hoseins first decided to carry out the kidnapping, two theories remain which may explain Mrs. McKay's death:

1. That she was kept in conditions which quickly had a harmful effect on her health. The shock of her capture, the rough handling, and finally exposure to extreme cold for two or three nights might well have precipitated the death from natural causes of a woman of fifty-five who had been used to a gentle, comfortable life.

2. That the kidnappers panicked when they found they had the wrong woman, and realising that the police were deeply involved in the case, murdered her.

Was Mrs. McKay killed at Rooks Farm? The police still think she was, although various people at the trial thought possibly not. The police believe that Rooks Farm provided the perfect spot for such nefarious work. Commander Guiver maintains this despite the fact that a number of people (including the local police, investigating a totally different matter) visited the farm during the early days of the enquiry. "All these people arrived unannounced," he commented. "The Hoseins were not to know beforehand that they were coming. Had the brothers been using another hide-out, I am sure that we would have discovered it. Men like that would have been conspicuous anywhere, and members of the public, reading about the case, would at some stage have realised who had moved in next door."

The trial judge chose to explain things differently: because outsiders were around the farm, he questioned, was it likely that Mrs. McKay was hidden there? This argument is strengthened by the fact that during these early days, a tailor friend of Arthur's telephoned, and was asked to come down to the farm. He was certainly an invited guest.

If Mrs. McKay did die at Rooks Farm, what happened to her body? The police were so perplexed that they could come up with no scientific evidence to support their theory, although they had—in their own words—"gone through the place with a toothcomb." Every conceivable hiding place, inside and outside the buildings, was examined. Over four thousand police man-hours were devoted to this aspect of the investigation alone. In fact, in the view of some of those associated, with the defence, this confirms the notion of the existence of another hiding place. They argue that although the police may not be very perceptive when dealing with crime in general, they have no equals when it comes to diligently following up a suggested line of enquiry. Why then could the prosecution produce no evidence to support their contention that Mrs. McKay had at some time been taken to Rooks Farm?

During the trial, reference was twice made to rumours that her body had been cut up and fed to the pigs. The idea is so horrific that one wonders whether even the Hosein brothers could have had the stomach for such an act. Yet it was a theory that detectives had to take seriously, for it was known that between the end of December and the middle of January, 1970, an animal had been slaughtered on the farm and its remains fed to the pigs. The Hoseins said it was a calf: the detectives had to ask themselves whether or not Mrs. McKay had been dismembered at the same time.

The police did not arrive at Rooks Farm until some six weeks after her disappearance, and it would have been quite possible in the interim for the brothers to have disposed of the remains. More than one hundred pig breeders and farmers phoned or wrote to Wimbledon police, telling Chief Superintendent Smith that pigs would readily eat a body, leaving only the large bones and hair, which could be burnt. One veterinary surgeon recounted a case where a man had fallen into the sty while feeding his pigs. When he was discovered, all that remained of him was part of an arm. (There was even a suggestion that this had been the method used to dispose of Frank Mitchell, the notorious "axe man" who escaped from Dartmoor Prison and has never been seen again.) Any bones left at Rooks Farm were sold to a man who called at irregular intervals to collect material for a local fertiliser factory, where they were ground up. In addition, it was impossible for the police to check the carcasses of the four pigs sold by the Hoseins early in the New Year for any trace of cortizone, the drug which Mrs. McKay had been taking.

The evidence in favour of the pigs theory disclosed by the police investigation was too insubstantial to be put to the jury. There was the hacksaw blade which had been borrowed around the time of Mrs. McKay's disappearance and which was later returned to its owner, completely blunt; similarly, the bill-hook lent to the Hoseins by a neighbouring farmer was found to have lost its cutting edge. There was also the story told by the owner of the Texan Leopard dog the day that both she and the dog had noticed a strange smell in the air coming from the direction of Rooks Farm, which reminded her instantly of burning bones. And finally there was the discovery of the remains of unidentifiable bones in the kitchen chimney at the farm.

All this was capable of innocent explanation: equally, it could all have added up to the conclusion that the Hoseins had first shot Mrs. McKay, then cut up her body, fed it to their pigs, and burnt the remains. The idea was reinforced by several reports of a lone shot being heard in the area during early January and by the discovery at Rooks Farm of a recently fired, double-barrelled shot gun with its ends inexplicably sawn down.

There was also the possibility that Mrs. McKay had been removed in one of the two ways favoured by professional liquidators—either by burial beneath the surface of a new road or motorway (it is rumoured that at least one of the victims of the London gang wars is now lying under the foundations of a London motor road) or by attaching a weight to the body and placing it in water. (It was only because the weights were incorrectly attached that another gangland victim eventually floated undecorously to the surface of the Channel near the seaside resort of Eastbourne.) Both methods have their disadvantages, because at some point those who are handling the body have to come into the open, and at first neither possibility was seriously considered. Then, while Nizam was on remand awaiting trial at Brixton prison, a fellow prisoner came forward to the authorities with an astonishing story.

This man, who was serving a sentence for forging cheques, said that while he and the younger Hosein were in the communal bath-house, he had asked, "How did you do it? What did you do with Mrs. McKay?" Nizam then told him that the body had been put in a reservoir near Windsor. The police later drained the reservoir, but found nothing. The man was never called as a witness at the trial because it was thought that his character and motive for telling the story would not have stood up under cross-examination. The defence could have implied that he had concocted the details of the conversation in the hope of gaining a remission or out of sheer bravado.

Was Nizam telling the truth on that occasion in the bath-house? Or was he just encouraging the adulation of his fellow-prisoners? The police placed their own "spy" in the prison in an attempt to draw out the Hoseins, but this move also failed. The Hoseins keep their secret for the moment: the McKay family do not even have the dubious comfort of knowing what happened, and the police have as yet been unable to "close the file" on the case.

Many financial inducements from newspapers, magazines, and television companies throughout Europe have been held out to the Hoseins to tell the full story. There were, and still are, many thousands of pounds available for the complete revelations. Commander Guiver considers that one day Arthur Hosein will tell the full story and reveal where the body was hidden or disposed of: "It would be completely within his character to seek this final boost to his ego."

Yet even without the precise knowledge which they would dearly have loved to possess, the government law enforcement officers were still able to bring a successful prosecution for murder. The jury's finding of guilt on the murder charge against both the Hosein brothers demolished forever the idea nurtured by some killers that without a body there could be no proof of crime. In fact there are a number of legal precedents for this course. Archbold's *Criminal Pleading*, the standard textbook in criminal practice, says of Absence of Body in murder and manslaughter proceedings, "The fact of death is provable by circumstantial evidence, notwithstanding that neither the body nor any trace of the body has been found and that the prisoner had made no confession of any participation in the crime.

"Before the prisoner can be convicted, the fact of death should be proved by such circumstances as render the commission of the crime certain and leave no ground for reasonable doubt. The circumstantial evidence should be so cogent and compelling as to convince a jury that on no rational hypothesis other than murder can the facts be accounted for."

Two hundred years ago the lawyer Sir Matthew Hale declared that he would never convict any person of murder or manslaughter "unless the fact were proved to be done, or at least the body found dead." But with the passing of time, the law has changed its view. Lord Goddard, when he was Lord Chief Justice, said that in today's changed conditions, where the evidence was strong enough, it would be very strange indeed were any court to decide that a murderer could not be convicted without production of the body.

In recent times there have been two cases before British courts where a murder conviction has resulted despite the absence of a body. James Camb, a steward on the liner Durban Castle, was found guilty of murdering the actress Gay Gibson while on the high seas in 1947, although Miss Gibson's body was never found. Here, the fact that Miss Gibson had been on board when the ship set sail from Cape Town, and was missing by the time the liner reached Southampton, was indisputable proof of her death: there was also evidence that Camb had been in her cabin just before she disappeared.

A case more reminiscent of that of Mrs. McKay was the murder of a Pole, Stanislaw Sykut, by a fellow-countryman, Michial Onufrejcyk. The men lived together on a lonely farm in the Welsh county of Carmarthenshire. One day Sykut disappeared, and although the police dug up the land and went through the house and outbuildings inch by inch, his body was never found. Onufrejcyzk was brought to trial in 1955 and found guilty, although he made no admission. Here too, there was a rumour that the victim had been fed to the pigs. Onufrejcyzk was sentenced to death, but on appeal against both conviction and sentence, the latter was commuted to life imprisonment. Onufrejcyzk's counsel, Elwyn Jones, Q.C. (later Sir Elwyn Jones, the Attorney General in the last Labour administration), maintained that unless the body could be found, or an account given of the death, there was no proof that a crime had been committed. That view was not accepted by the Appeal Court: Lord Goddard said death, like any other fact, could be proved by circumstantial evidence which led to only one conclusion.

Many of the audience at the trial of the Hoseins—legal pundits as well as laymen—would have been prepared to wager that the brothers stood a good chance of getting off the murder charge. To the onlooker, it seemed that the counts of murder had been put there more to tidy up the prosecution story than from any real hope of a conviction. After all, was the circumstantial evidence "so cogent and compelling" as Archbold suggests it should be? Of kidnapping, threatening to kill and demanding money with menaces, it was. As to murder, the certainty that the brothers had abducted Mrs. McKay led the jury's mind irrevocably to the conclusion that they were involved in her murder. The issue could have gone either way: in favour of the Hoseins ("Where's the body? Where's the proof?") or to the Attorney General ("They abducted her, Q.E.D. they killed her"). In the end, perhaps, it was not so much a case of the prosecution winning as of the Hoseins defeating themselves. Their performances in court were enough to strain anyone's faith in their scarcely credible fantasies. They fell out with each other, Arthur fell out with the court and Nizam spoke so softly—even with a microphone round his neck—that one was bound to jump to the conclusion that he was attempting to disguise his voice. After all, it was he who was alleged to have made most of the ransom calls, in the guise of M3, to the McKay family.

In court Arthur Hosein seemed quite unaware of the gravity of his situation. By turns he was bombastic and funny in the witness box. At one stage when the Attorney General lost his place in the mass of witnesses' statements, Arthur rebuked him: "Come, come, Mr. Attorney General, you can do better than that." When he was asked to hand an exhibit on to the jury, Arthur told the foreman, "Don't be afraid. I'm not dangerous."

Which was the dominant partner? Whose was the mind which first conceived the crime? The third man theory aside, each of the Hoseins has his supporters and detractors. The police certainly think that Arthur was the one whose brain created the monster. However, he had made a good living for himself and his wife and children in England. There was the tailoring business, the farm in the country, and the two cars: the recognised symbols of success in our affluent society. It was a mode of life that was to crumble only when Nizam arrived on the scene. At about the time the kidnap plot was first considered Nizam was about to be expelled from Britain on the expiration of his three months visa. This predicament could have been the catalyst which turned Arthur's dreams of great wealth and prestige into a tangible form. It would be unwise to regard Nizam as nothing more than the puppet under his elder brother's dominance.

Someone who knew both the brothers said he believed Arthur was thought guilty of many of Nizam's sins. "Nizam is a very intelligent 'idiot'—he pretends he can't understand, can't hear too well and is a bit slow on the uptake. Arthur was the terrier, Nizam the big dog. Arthur could yap harder and stronger and make the big fellow bow down: but his bark wasn't as bad as the other man's bite.

"We know Nizam made most of the calls to the McKays' house. There would be occasions when the brothers were out on business, delivering trousers around the East End, when Nizam would get out of the car on the pretext of buying a bottle of beer, a packet of cigarettes, or of calling his girlfriend—and at the same time pop into a street corner phone box to put in another call to Arthur Road. It was as if the distinction between normal and abnormal acts had never existed for him."

The police, whose view of an accused person tends to be restricted by the narrow question of his guilt or innocence, think that Arthur may have been the chief conspirator and that Nizam was nothing more than a willing tool in the plot. A strange story that came to light after the trial suggests that this may be true. On the first of the two occasions when the police unsuccessfully set a trap baited with half a million pounds in forged five pound notes, the Hoseins slipped through. On their way back to the farm in their car, the brothers had an argument which ended with Nizam being turned out into the rain by Arthur, and told to make his own way home. Arthur then drove off and, being a great womaniser, picked up a girl in Bishop's Stortford. Nizam eventually arrived home at about three o'clock in the morning, looking like a drowned rat.

Again one must ask whether these were really the "masterminds," the men who had led a family, a police force, and a nation by the nose for seven weeks. Or were they two poseurs who by turns were capable of reaching great depths of criminal deviousness and of making laughable errors? Grabbing Mrs. McKay and spiriting her away unnoticed took resource and nerve, yet at the same time the Hoseins left behind at St. Mary House a host of clues. Was this an example of twisted minds at work? Did they want to leave behind an embarrassment of evidence for the police in order to confuse them (for that is certainly what happened)? It seems scarcely possible, yet perhaps the Hoseins saw themselves as master criminals, pitting their superior mentalities against the plodding orthodoxy of the police mind.

Some of their actions were so stupid that the question that inevitably comes to mind is "Why didn't the police catch them sooner?" The first telephone call demanding one million pounds in ransom money for Mrs. McKay was made from a public telephone box. The kidnappers were unable to obtain the right number, so they got through to the operator, asking him to connect them. The use of the Hoseins' own Volvo car led back to them in the end. Yet Arthur Hosein had many contacts in the East End; it would not have been difficult for him to have obtained the use of a car with false number plates. Then there was the astonishing journey that Nizam made within a few hours of the kidnapping, back into the district around Wimbledon. Flashing a roll of money that could only have come from Mrs. McKay (Nizam never had had any money of his own), he repaid an insignificant debt to his brother Adam and then went on to see his cousin, Sharif Mustapha. What prompted such a visit at that particular moment? The detectives believe that the real reason may have been Arthur's desire to know exactly what was happening at Arthur Road: with that in mind, he sent Nizam down in the Volvo, on the pretext of calling on his relations. There was little chance of Nizam being noticed as he drove past the McKays' house that night, but all the same it was a rash move and one that a professional criminal would never have made. It also indicated once again the degree to which Nizam appears to have been working under Arthur's instructions. If it had been left up to him, the younger Hosein would probably never have chosen to risk being discovered back at the scene of the crime on the night it had been committed.

This question of risk may be the answer to another of the puzzles surrounding the case: Why was this Britain's first ever kidnapping? Was it because, in this type of crime, the odds of success are too heavily loaded against the criminal? The sixties were an era when crime had become truly international in both concept and practice: Great Train Robbery money had found its way into speculative businesses across the Atlantic, and Martin Luther King's assassin was arrested in London. Yet until 29th December, 1969, kidnapping was a crime which was quite alien to the ordinary Englishman. If most people in the United Kingdom had heard of Lindbergh or Peugeot it was as aviator and carmaker, not as the victims of kidnapping.

Why had Britain never experienced it before? The criminal the world over is quick to spot a crime that offers high financial returns and the British criminal is no more scrupulous about the type of work to which he turns his hand than his American, Japanese, or European counterparts: he is no less greedy, ambitious, or able. It has been suggested that kidnapping is an operation for professional gangs, such as the Mafia, and argued that as Britain had no gangs to speak of until the Krays and the Richardsons* came on the scene, we as a nation were not vulnerable to that particular type of crime. Yet, if one excludes southern Italy, where the strength of the Mafia is such that kidnapping is a paying proposition, nearly all abductions are carried out by a handful of young men (often with the aid of a girl-friend) who are out to get rich. And they are almost always incapable of assessing the likelihood of success or failure beforehand. The chances of picking up the money, escaping the police, and disappearing undetected to a different country are very much loaded against the would-be kidnapper. It is a crime where the perpetrator is asking for trouble. He runs extreme risk on three separate occasions—taking the victim, collecting the money, and returning his prize. All the time he is dealing with the one commodity over which he can never have complete control—a human being. In an emergency, stolen property can always be hidden or destroyed. It is not so simple with a captive man, woman, or child.

If criminals were ever to work on a cost analysis basis, they would realise that if the amount of time spent and the risk taken were to be set against their potential earnings, the end product was likely to be very little indeed. The ransom payment of $600,000 for Robert C. (Bobby) Greenlease bears out this point. Greenlease was kidnapped in September 1953 and the child's body was found at St. Joseph, Missouri, ten days later. His family paid the ransom, but the kidnappers, Carl Austin Hall and Mrs. Bonnie Brown, did not have long to enjoy their windfall. They were caught and sentenced to death. Five hundred thousand dollars (£205,000) seems to be the asking price in America these days: elsewhere demands are far more modest. In Japan, France, and Germany, countries where there has been a rash of kidnappings during the last decade, the ransom demand has varied from as little as £500 up to a ceiling of £50,000.

Many crimes such as bomb hoaxes are imitative, and there

---

* Two London mobs of the 1960s who brought extortion, intimidation, torture, and murder to the capital. It was the first time Britain had ever experienced organized crime on this scale.

may be something in the argument that kidnapping was un-known in Britain prior to the McKay case simply because it had never happened there before. Again, bearing in mind the internationalism of crime, it is curious to note that after the Hoseins, Austria, too, in 1970 found itself confronted with its first kidnapping. There, the twenty-five-year-old heir to a con-fectionery fortune was freed and his captors arrested after a ransom of £5,000 had been paid.

This indeed is the pattern which the detection of kidnapping is following: the police step out of the case while the family make a deal with the kidnappers. Then, when the money has been paid and the victim returned, the police re-enter the in-vestigation. In France, Germany, and America, this policy has been doubly vindicated on several occasions, both by the safe return of the victim and the subsequent arrest of the crimi-nals. Even when the kidnapper is allowed this concession, the flaws in his crime are many and his chances of remaining free to enjoy the illicit rewards are few: the victim will be able to provide evidence about where he was held and the kind of vehicle in which he was taken, and the money may be traced back to the spenders. Kidnapping is indeed an exaggeratedly dangerous game of Russian roulette for the perpetrator. As the McKay case showed, the criminal's chances of escape are in inverse ratio to the time he spends carrying out the deal: if the exchange is made within two or three days, he has a gambler's chance of success. But when it is spread over weeks, as the Hoseins chose to work, the prospects of avoiding the police are negligible. Unhappily, so too are the chances of the victim's survival. If kidnappers must act quickly, the police must react with the same speed. In this case, Mrs. McKay was killed.

7
THE LESSON
TO BE LEARNT

Who Was On Trial?

ONE OF THE drawbacks of the English trial system is that it limits itself to the question of guilt or innocence. Often issues are raised in a case that fail to receive an airing because the court takes the view that they are outside its competence.

In the Hoseins' trial, the overriding theme appeared to be the law's desire for retribution—a prisoner for a prisoner—when there were other issues equally pertinent to the affair that were never discussed. They can perhaps be summed up in two questions:

1. Could Mrs. McKay have been saved once she had fallen into the hands of the Hoseins?
2. What lessons have been learnt in the event of another kidnapping?

To try to answer these points, it is necessary to look at the roles of the police, the press, and the McKay family, and to consider, in retrospect, whether their parts in the affair could be faulted. (Some might add a fourth party to the case—the criminals themselves. But it is not really possible to analyse their actions in this respect. The functions of the other three groups and their reactions to the situation in which they were caught are capable of examination and debate.)

An analysis of the way the affair unfolded shows that to an extent all three parties were siding with or against each other at some stage; one of the extraordinary features of the case was this three-sided tug-o'-war, with Mrs. McKay the unfortunate victim in the middle. For a long time too, all three groups were puppets whose strings were being jerked first this way and then that by the malevolent puppet-masters, the Hoseins. As Chief Superintendent Smith told *The Times* after the case, "The kidnappers held the initiative from the start. They held the whip hand and knew it."

The Federal Bureau of Investigation, whose experience of kidnapping cases is unsurpassed, says that after three or four days in captivity a victim's chances of coming out alive are almost nil: if by then no deal has been made they are too much of a liability to their captors to be allowed to remain alive. Police statistics from the United States have shown that 70 per cent of kidnap victims die within the first forty-eight hours. There is circumstantial evidence that things were happening at Rooks Farm on 1st January which could have been connected with Mrs. McKay's death. In the absence of certain knowledge, the police have estimated that she did on that day, a Thursday. (Mrs. Else Hosein and her children were due back from their holiday in Germany within a couple of days, which made it all the more necessary to remove the evidence.) Therefore, from the moment that M3 made the first telephone call from the Bell Common box at 1:15 A.M. on 30th December, there was a maximum of about two days in which to arrange for Mrs. McKay's safe return.

Could some deal have been made in those forty-eight hours? As the case unfolded it became clear that for three reasons Mrs. McKay's chances were virtually nil. There was the impossibility of raising one million pounds in so short a time; the reluctance of the Hoseins, or their inability to talk about business arrangements; and the fact that they failed to leave a ransom note at St. Mary House when they took Mrs. McKay.

It has been said with some force that the British police were inexperienced in crimes of kidnapping and that this ignorance held them back; ironically, it could be presumed that the Hoseins' total ignorance of what to do once they had got their victim led to Mrs. McKay's death. If they had left behind a ransom demand the whole affair might have taken a very different course. Perhaps they brought one with them to the house, but finding they had got the wrong woman were thrown into confusion. However implausible their scheme, the Hoseins were in this for money; it seems likely it was this circumstance which turned them into murderers.

156

So, because of the errors committed by one of the two parties to a prospective deal, Mrs. McKay's chances of surviving were very slight. But on the other side as well a positive "attitude of mind" was equally necessary—a realisation by the police that this was a kidnapping and, just as quickly, a decision on how to get Mrs. McKay back unharmed. The police say their first priority was to get her back safely and nobody disputes that. But by the time they were close to the Hoseins they were pretty certain she was already dead. Thus the priority was really only an academic one.

Bearing the American experience in mind, did the police in this case respond quickly enough to ensure Mrs. McKay's safety? What separates a kidnapping from other crimes is the extra dimension it contains for the investigators. Not only is there the problem of detection and conviction of the criminals, there is the very delicate moral issue of whether the rules should be bent in the interests of the victim.

Well within the forty-eight hour "limit of survival" the police had an abundance of evidence pointing to this being a kidnapping case. For various reasons, which we will examine, it took them all that time to decide that kidnapping was the probable explanation; for some days after they were still actively considering other reasons for her disappearance.

Before suggesting where police strategy and attitudes may have gone awry in the vital early days of the case, two points must be borne in mind which help to explain the plight of the detectives. One was the actions of the Hoseins, behaving like anything but kidnappers. But equally there was the mystery of the chain on the outer door of St. Mary House, something that has never been satisfactorily explained. How did the Hoseins get past that barrier, especially since Mrs. McKay was still nervous after the robbery three months before and was not likely to open the door to strange coloured men? (Some people have spoken of seeing marks of some sort on the outer door, but it has never been seriously suggested that the chain was forced.)

There is the possibility that Mrs. McKay, having returned home and expecting her husband in for dinner, herself left the chain off. But this was the middle of the winter, it was dark and Alick McKay was not due for another two hours.

Discounting that theory and being left with a complete riddle, it is understandable the police should come up at first with only one hypothesis—that Mrs. McKay took the chain off herself to someone she knew well. Did this suggest that her "abductor" was a close friend? Or Mr. McKay himself? A small issue but terribly important for the police. If it could have been cleared up at the start, the way would have been open to the police to take a more positive line from the night of 29th December.

The Police

When criminals make errors, they are usually easy meat for an experienced policeman. But the more the Hoseins tripped up, the more confused the police became.

The scene discovered by Alick McKay when he returned to Arthur Road from work on the Monday evening was so suggestive of someone being taken away by force that the police set their minds against the idea. It was all too neatly set up, they reasoned. There was string to bind the hands, sticking plaster to seal the lips and eyes, a weapon to threaten with, signs of "orderly disorder" as if someone had carefully strewn articles about the hall and stairs, and a rifling of the bedroom which did not suggest the work of a determined burglar.

If the police at that time had other thoughts, one predominated: that Mrs. McKay had set this up herself. Then why? Because she wanted to make it appear a crime had been committed when she had disappeared freely—perhaps with another man. (To the detectives this was not unknown, particularly in the case of women in their late forties and early fifties.) Yet all the time the truth was being shouted at the detectives from each and every piece of evidence. *That was at eight o'clock on the night of 29th December.*

All the time there was Alick McKay assuring the police his wife was not the kind of person to go off like this. He told the same story to everyone who had time to listen: his home life had been happy, there were no medical reasons and no "other men" in her life. McKay could read the truth from the evidence scattered around. Yet nobody heeded him. Instead he was the number one suspect! His unusually collected manner and the fact that it had taken him fifteen minutes to call the police coloured this view. In addition, experience told the detectives that he, as the husband and complainant in the case, was the statistical favourite. When McKay and the evidence were both pointing to the truth, the police had it in their mind that the criminal might be sitting there in the deep armchair at St. Mary House talking to them. *That was by ten o'clock on the night of 29th December.*

At 1:15 A.M. the following morning came the first artless and clumsy contact between M3 and the family: the phone call that had to be put through via an operator who overheard part of the conversation. That call demanded one million pounds by the Wednesday, two days later, or Mrs. McKay would die. Her husband was to await instructions for the payment. Even allowing for the abnormalities of the kidnappers' behaviour, the case was following the normal progression in such a crime: abduction—ransom demand—threats on the victim's life—the date for the exchange named—instructions to await further orders. *That was at 1:15 A.M. on 30th December.*

But the police were now more suspicious than ever. The whole manner of the approach had been wrong: the use of an open line through an operator, even giving their number. Criminals did not indulge in such follies. And the demand for one million pounds! McKay had not got that kind of money and no sane person could expect him to raise it, let alone within two days.

What a tragedy! If the police had accepted the call at its face value, might Mrs. McKay be alive today? Instead the detectives were firmly convinced that the call was not genuine but a hoax. If the call was not from the kidnappers, who else outside the family circle knew Mrs. McKay was missing; who would play such a sick joke? This is where the strands of Fleet Street and the McKay family became intertwined for the first time in the police machinery, an issue to be considered separately. It is enough for the moment to say that the police at that stage had grave suspicions about the involvement of someone or some newspaper in Mrs. McKay's disappearance— another suspicion which proved to be completely groundless.

Later that afternoon, M3 put through another call, this time to David Dyer, with the ominous warning, "for her sake don't call the police." By then the tape-recorder had been set up at the house to keep track of all phone messages, but the police still retained an open mind about M3's genuineness. Finally, on 31st December, the first letter from Mrs. McKay arrived, posted in North London the previous evening. Even then the police were not excluding the possibility that the letter might have been a blind by Mrs. McKay to draw them off the scent. Awaiting confirmation from the police laboratories, Smith accepted the family's word that it was their mother's writing. But where were the arrangements for the ransom? And how much were they now asking? This letter did not even carry the M3 "call sign." At all events *by nine o'clock on the morning of Wednesday, 31st December, it was known she was a prisoner.*

The police say that by New Year's Eve they were convinced Mrs. McKay had been abducted; that it was the letter which made up their minds for them. Other people who met them at the house claim that it was between eight and ten days before the detectives gave up the idea she had gone off voluntarily (although those at the house did not know it, it was certainly that long before Alick McKay himself was finally freed of suspicion).

Recognition of the authenticity of the letter and the second phone call was further complicated by the welter of false and malicious messages; it is easy enough to react to one ransom message, but when it is only one of dozens, the process of weeding out slows the investigation.

Many other factors emanate from the delay in recognising the symptoms of a kidnapping case. But it must be said in defence of the police that it is often wiser not to rush to a conclusion. In the first forty-eight hours at least, the detectives were still weighing up the options. Training and experience teaches a detective to keep an open mind. Once he has formed a definite view there is always the danger that any facts which turn up later will be made to fit that view. For the sake of detection—indeed for the benefit of an innocent person—this is entirely the right attitude. But again, kidnapping poses special problems not easily reconciled with normal processes of investigation and deduction.

One difficulty which faces the detective in such a crime is that he is always on the defensive. It is the kidnapper who dictates the course an enquiry takes, who issues the orders family and police must follow. Here, the police did try to take the initiative by seeking to draw out the kidnappers with a false story of Mrs. McKay's health. Unhappily that failed; in any case the attempt came too late to be of any consequence to the issue of saving her life.

But there was an opportunity for the detectives within the two day "survival limit" which, if used, could have brought the Hoseins out into the open in time for Mrs. McKay to be rescued. If Alick McKay, when faced with the demand over the telephone at 1:15 that Tuesday morning, had responded "positively" by saying he could get the million pounds, this might successfully have laid the bait for the criminals. Of course, McKay ("I haven't got anything like a million") was responding instinctively to the suggestion. And the police, having little idea at that stage that it was a kidnapping, had not taken the trouble to prime him on his answers. (An important feature of the later stages of the enquiry was that Ian McKay was carefully coached about his replies.)

But the opportunity to trap the kidnappers with the million pounds bait did present itself on the afternoon of 30th December when the Hoseins rang again at 4:59 P.M. This time, when David Dyer was asked by M3 "Did you get the money?" a positive answer might have whetted their avaricious appetites.

On this day—Tuesday, 30th December—the police were still in two minds: they were not yet inclined to give the kidnapping theory much credence, although they were recording all phone calls. It must be remembered too that to trap M3 with the prospect of one million pounds, the co-operation of the family was necessary. At that stage Smith had not yet established a rapport with the McKay clan.

In fact the friction between the police and the family over the whole question of publicity for the case had then reached its peak. In the succeeding days, Chief Superintendent Smith was able to come to terms with the McKays in their desperation and they with him in his resolve not to rush the case.

But in those early days the press, in the eyes of Smith, Guiver, and the other detectives, had committed two unforgiveable sins: it had stirred up publicity to such a degree that the response by phone to St. Mary House and Wimbledon police station had made the investigation almost unmanageable, and the manner of press publicity had grossly hindered the work of the detectives. If one grants a forty-eight hour time limit for achieving Mrs. McKay's safe return, what specifically had the press (and radio and television) done wrong, from the police point of view?

1. A statement had gone out to the Press Association on the first evening, 29th December, which alerted the world to Mrs. McKay's disappearance. This story was carried in the later editions of the next morning's newspapers and the BBC mentioned it in its 1 A.M. news bulletin on 30th December. Fifteen minutes later, M3 made the first telephone call to the McKay house but, because of the publicity the disappearance had already received, the police did not believe M3, thinking instead the call was the work of a hoaxer who had heard or read the news.

2. The phones to the house and to Wimbledon police station were soon besieged with malicious and well-intentioned callers and with the press themselves. Because of this the kidnappers were unable to make their wishes known even if they had wanted to.

3. The contents of the letter from Mrs. McKay which arrived at Arthur Road on 31st December were fully published after the police had decided against any mention of the letter.

There were other, more general, issues resulting from McKay's position as a newspaper executive which also tended to sidetrack the police during this period. When the police began to assemble at St. Mary House, they found the editor of the *Sun*, Larry Lamb, one of his reporters and a photographer already there. Immediately the police were suspicious, and one can understand their reasoning without necessarily agreeing with them. The new *Sun* had been going for just six weeks and was thirsty for circulation; it thrived on sensation as all mass-circulation papers must; here were the editor and two of his men at the house of a senior executive whose wife had just gone missing in strange circumstances. In all, it seemed more than pure coincidence. Policemen and journalists are by nature suspicious of one another. If Fleet Street later thought the police were being unduly cautious over the case, some police minds were beginning to see the hand of the press in the spiriting away of Mrs. McKay. The way the *Sun* splashed the story that first morning ("Mystery of Press Chief's Vanished Wife") only confirmed the suspicion that it might be a publicity stunt that had got out of hand. Perhaps this shows the unworldliness of the police when it comes to dealing with the press. Those who work in the industry know just how inconceivable is such a suggestion. "Kidnap" a pop star or a race-horse: such stunts are just about feasible with the connivance of the "victims." But newspapers, whatever dashing image they may give to the public, are the most ultra-convservative of organisations when it comes to dealing with their own affairs. Nobody who wants to hold onto his job is going to suggest, let alone put into practice, the kidnapping of one of his own senior executives' wives as a circulation-boosting peep-show.

The police also had to consider whether Mrs. McKay had been taken as a tool in a vendetta against the *News of the World*, again a paper that grows fat on sensation. Of course the police had to consider every angle, however unlikely, but McKay was a backroom boy in the organisation, far removed from the glamour of the editorial pages. He had arrived at the *News of the World* only five weeks before and if the public had ever come across his name, which is doubtful, they certainly would not have identified him with the "exposé" qualities of the paper. It was much more likely that the kidnap victim would have been the then editor, Stafford Somerfield.

But one must sympathise with the police in their predicament. The fact that the chief character in the case was a man capable of considerable influence in fields where the police service feels itself especially vulnerable to scrutiny was to have an unfortunately complicating effect on the enquiry. As one journalist commented, "The police needed a newspaper executive as the complainant about as much as they wanted a hole in their heads. You take anyone else, anyone off the street and they wouldn't know what to do. They would just say, 'You're the coppers, you're paid to do it, you find my wife.' But a journalist picks up a phone. . . . And the bigger a wheel he is the more numbers he can dial."

To say that the police were to some extent railroaded into activity by outside pressure is not to imply that they are at the beck and call of every politico and newspaper orator. But policemen have the civil servant's attitude: if there is the slightest chance of criticism at any stage, be sure you at least have done your job. Then the blame can only fall on somebody else's head. So, when a very senior Scotland Yard officer is rung at midnight on 29th December by an equally senior Fleet Street executive to ask what has happened to Mrs. McKay, and is reminded of her husband's prominence and that nobody seems to be taking him seriously, is it any wonder that Wimbledon police station is soon beginning to jump?

The three specific police complaints against the mass media are dealt with later in the section on the role of the press, but a further question which falls into the forty-eight-hour time-limit remains to be answered. How would the police have acted had they reached the stage where money was to be exchanged for Mrs. McKay?

Here one is up against the intractability of the police mind in Britain. If society gets the police force it deserves, then that force is a reflection of society's views. Where a society such as this has been hurt, it looks to its police force to demonstrate its feelings of disapproval and anger. In the McKay case, law and order had been outraged and demanded revenge. Understandable feelings, these, except that in crimes such as kidnappings revenge must be a secondary consideration: here the first was the safe return of an innocent woman.

Commander Guiver said later in the investigation that it would not have been possible for the police to back out and allow the family to bargain separately with the kidnappers for Mrs. McKay's life. His belief—which is certainly shared by the vast majority of policemen—is that to have done so would make a mockery of law and order and would invite further kidnappings. (Though the authors disagree with this view, it is only fair to state that within the year following the Hoseins' arrest there were no further kidnappings, although it is a crime which is open to imitation.)

164

Commander Guiver did concede, however, that if there was another kidnapping he thought the authorities might have to consider an independent negotiating committee, as was done in recent political kidnappings, notably the case of the British diplomat, Mr. James Cross, and the Quebec FLQ. "But even there the police were always hovering in the background. Once they are in on it, you just cannot keep the police out of an investigation."

Not even if it meant the difference between life and death for the victim? "Then what happens when she is found dead anyway and your family has paid over the money? It is the policeman who will get the blame."

Chief Superintendent Smith told *The Times* that the police "have learnt a lot during the last nine months. We may have made a few mistakes but we faced a crime which had never been committed in this country before. There was no precedent, nothing we could fall back on to help us."

Here Smith implied that ignorance of this kind of crime did handicap the investigators. While the routine of police investigation does not vary much from crime to crime, it was in failing to understand from the very start the psychology of a kidnapping that the detectives showed their inexperience of the offence.

Should not the police be able to anticipate new forms of crime by preparing for them? Scotland Yard has recognized the need for some form of pre-planning by creating a small headquarters unit which would be responsible for plane hijackings and political kidnappings; criminal kidnappings such as the McKay case would also fall to this unit to investigate. Here lies the hope that in a future police kidnapping enquiry, inexperience or ignorance of the crime will no longer be a handicap.

When a member of the McKay family made the tentative suggestion to the police that they let the McKays make a straight deal—"no strings, no police"—for the return of their mother, it was greeted with stony disapproval by the detectives. Again the orthodoxy of the British police mind could not swallow the thought of making deals with criminals. (When one brilliant and unorthodox Yard officer did exactly that in order to catch much bigger fry, his methods engendered only bitterness amongst some of his colleagues.*) In the words of one Metropolitan Police detective, "The Yard is never exactly receptive to advice from outside. Its view was that if it couldn't handle the McKay kidnappers, nobody could; certainly not amateurs like the family."

If the British police have learnt nothing else, they must now realise that when dealing with a kidnapper, society has to be prepared to "sup with the devil" if its first priority is the safe return of the victim. Here we can learn much from other countries. In the FBI "bible," the agent is told that his primary concern is the victim's safety. As one of the Bureau's officers commented, "We would never do anything to jeopardise that principle. We would permit the family to do any deal they wished."

The FBI has a twenty-four-hour "presumptive" clause in its mandate which enables it to enter a case in any state after one day on the probability that the case is now a federal crime—kidnapping or interstate transportation. In practice, the Bureau is even closer to the crime: it enters the investigation on a watching brief from the moment an alert is issued, maintaining liaison with state, county, or city police until its help is officially sought.

In the FBI's view, early publicity—by which it means the three or four days at the beginning when a deal can be made to get the victim back—is enough to ruin the whole operation. In America, says the Bureau, most newspaper editors are willing to co-operate, although after a week or so they start straining at the leash. "The less the publicity, the better are your chances of getting him or her back. Once the publicity starts, your kidnapper gets worked up too and that isn't good for the victim. When there's nothing on the television or in the papers, it keeps your kidnapper in the dark. Publicity certainly hampered the British police and didn't do Mrs. McKay much good."

---

* To trap the Kray gang, Leonard "Nipper" Read was allowed to use unorthodox methods. His success brought with it the jealousy of other officers. Read later left the Yard to take a high appointment with a provincial police force.

In Smith's view, the six-and-a-half weeks it took to confront the Hoseins could have been reduced to seven or ten days but for the interference of the media.

Apart from the issue of press culpability, the FBI view—which must be respected because of the Bureau's long experience in such cases—underlines the necessity for the police to come to a very early diagnosis on a kidnapping. If Scotland Yard, on the evidence available to them after the 1:15 A.M. phone call on 30th December, had put out a "Stop" message to editors on the McKay story and had followed it up the next morning with a full, confidential background briefing, all early publicity could have been stifled. (One problem here was that the McKay family themselves were keen on publicity; but if they had been taken fully into the Yard's confidence, they too presumably would have seen the wisdom of silence.)

The police may ask how, once they had been called into the case, they were going to get out of it in order to allow the McKays to deal directly with M3. The answer is that they could for once have turned the mass media to their own advantage by announcing to the world that for a set time they were willing to withdraw. A desperate measure perhaps, but the situation demanded desperate remedies. Such a method was effectively used by the Paris police in a famous kidnapping case in 1960: the abduction of Eric Peugeot, four-year-old grandson of the head of the giant car firm. In that enquiry too the family tried to get the police out of the investigation, and the police refused. But such was the power of the Peugeot name that in the end the detectives were ordered to stand aside until £35,000 had been paid over and the child returned unharmed.

The prevalence of political kidnappings has led many governments and law enforcement agencies to consider what their attitudes will be when they are faced with this kind of blackmail. Some have shown a willingness to negotiate, others an obdurate refusal. What Scotland Yard and the Home Office should have learnt from the McKay case is that rules and procedures must be pliable enough to allow room for manoeuvre if there is to be a chance of the victim's safe return.

If the authorities remain determined to see crime investigation and detection purely as a deterrent—to the possible detriment of the victim—they may lose the confidence of the public. This is one reason why many people today prefer to take their problems to a private detective agency. They do not fear the police, only the consequences of getting involved in the machinery of law: once the wheels are set in motion it is almost impossible to switch them off.

Whatever happened after 1st January could not affect Mrs. McKay's fate. But the machinery of the police investigation is worthy of a closer analysis.

At the end of the Hoseins' trial, the judge praised Chief Superintendent Smith and his team for a piece of "brilliant detective work." Cumulatively, it was certainly impressive, though not one of those cases where one could point to a single policeman and say, "He cracked it," or put one's hand on an isolated clue and say, "That clinched it." Above all it was a triumph of organisation and persistence, and that is the way major crimes are solved today. If the police are criticised for their mis-management at the Dane End ransom drop, the efficient manner in which some eighty men were deployed on the night of the rendezvous at Gates Garage is worthy of inclusion in any handbook of military strategy.

The day of the maverick detective, working by instinct, has largely disappeared, as has his image as a man in a dirty grey macintosh with a trilby and a scruffy old suit. Organisation and uniformity, a dark suit and a white collar have taken over. As major crime becomes more of a matter of organisation and planning, so investigation and detection demands the same businesslike approach. Only in this way have the police been able to keep pace with the increase in crime. But uniformity has certain drawbacks: it discourages the thinker, the man with imagination and flair (the authors know of at least two Scotland Yard detectives who, having reached a high rank at an early age, resigned because they felt the service was not utilising their abilities—a complaint not peculiar to the police). If the McKay case lacked anything, it was this intuitive feeling by the police that would have enabled them to have summed up the situation from the start.

An American policeman, taking very much the "policeman's view" of the case ("dog does not eat dog" is an adage which applies very much in the international freemasonry of the service) said, "I reckon they did a hell of a good job: after all, they got a conviction, didn't they?" That was taking the narrow view. Less fulsome was the response of an experienced daily newspaper crime correspondent: "Brilliant? I would call it brave, bearing in mind all the problems that they had, not just of finding the Hoseins, but also the pressure they were under from the Yard hierarchy. They were battered from pillar to post at some stages by senior officers and they were very courageous to stick it out. But as far as detective work went, that was not particularly outstanding: rather more a gradual building up."

A "good pinch" then, achieved in the face of overwhelming odds, not the least of which was the service's innate conservatism. For instance, the tape-recorder had to be brought from a detective's home because it would have taken too long to get one through official channels. (Normally, it is an offence to attach any instrument to a telephone in order to record a conversation; the police had to get formal permission from the Post Office to stick their suction pad on the phone in St. Mary House.)

Then, when the police wanted a helicopter, they had to borrow one with the help of the *News of the World*. That London, one of the largest cities in the world, does not have a single police helicopter is a matter for incredulity among American police forces. The keepers of police monies are not yet convinced that a machine (a two-seater costs about £22,000 and a five-seater £60,000) would repay the financial outlay. Yet even if their use in crime detection is of necessity limited, there is still the job of traffic control and observation from the air. Scotland Yard and the Home Office have at last agreed to set up a ten-man helicopter observation team, but even here the authorities have reached a penny-pinching compromise. If a helicopter is needed it will be hired, and so will the civilian pilot. In the short run, there may be a saving to the tax-payer and the rate-payer, but in the long term the public may well find themselves spending more on hire charges than if one machine had been bought outright.

In the later stages of the McKay enquiry, the police were to show welcome signs of a willingness to go beyond the tried and tested detective measures which then appeared to be having little effect and to venture into less conventional areas. It took some nerve, for instance, for Smith and Guiver to set up the plan for printing nearly half a million pounds in forged fivers. The Bank of England, when it got to hear what had gone on, was not at all happy. But the police were able to assure the bank authorities that there was no danger of the forged money ever being passed as real currency; in any case the notes were shredded under police supervision after the arrests.

Then there was the use of the homing device and the attempt to use the new science of voice-printing to catch the kidnappers. Some older policemen would say the detectives were driven into the arms of science by their own inability to get the case moving. But this is just the kind of attitude that handicaps the service. Professor Francis Camps, the world-renowned pathologist and criminologist, has spent much of his own time trying to convince the British police and the Home Office of the value of testing the American lie-detectors. The Americans were even willing to lend one free of charge, but the Home Office, on police advice, declined. Camps is one of the few disciples of the lie-detector, or polygraph, in Britain. He believes that under the polygraph the Hoseins might have revealed the secret of the whereabouts of Mrs. McKay. Whether or not this is true, mistrust of science-based methods of detection still prodominates in many police minds.

There were many times as they tried to get close to the kidnappers when the police must have felt they were playing snakes and ladders, and that they were going down the board more often than up. It was Smith's skilful handling of the McKay family which was central to the final success: first getting them to overcome their doubts about the helpfulness of a police action, then winning their active support, and finally enlisting the help of Ian McKay in playing up to M3 on the phone.

The courage of the men who went out into the unknown on the ransom drops cannot be overlooked. They had no way of telling whether the criminals would really be armed with guns or coshes (one of the younger officers drank five large brandies in as many minutes to fortify himself for one rendezvous). Inspector Minors bore the brunt of the work.

"He was not to know if he was walking into a hornet's nest. It showed the man's nerve that he went without demurring," said one journalist who is not particularly pro-police.

But the detectives were lucky to be able to lay the ransom trap for the Hoseins twice. After the mistakes at Dane End, they could really not have complained had M3 just taken fright and disappeared. The vulnerability of police radio wave-lengths—not only to journalists' informants but to the criminals themselves—has long been recognized. What was even worse was the ham-handed manner of the police on surveillance on the road that night, something that may have been due in part to rivalry between various squads. That the Hoseins were later able to tell Ian McKay in their melo-dramatic way, "The boss laughed and said he had seen cars around the pick-up spot" was an indictment of the way the operation was carried out, as was the ease with which the brothers were able to spot a car-load of detectives at a transport cafe a few hundred yards from where the money was waiting.

Then, a week later, while Inspector Minors, dressed as Alick McKay, was standing in the phone box in Bethnal Green, he too was being scrutinised by the Hoseins from a distance of only two hundred yards. The police believed Minors and Woman Dective-Constable Armitage, posing as Diane Dyer, were not being watched, for Minors was told after some debate back at the operations centre that it was safe for him to drive towards Epping instead of taking the tube at Bethnal Green as instructed. So an hour later at the Epping station call-box, Minors was told by M3, "I see you are being watched."

Whether the Hoseins knew for certain the police were present or whether they were only guessing will never be known. What *is* known is that the police were sure the ex-change was going to be one way only: the money but no Mrs. McKay. But if there was even the remotest hope that she was still alive, her continued existence could have been endangered by the kidnappers' realisation that they had walked into a trap.

The difficulties of arranging protection for the decoy Mc-Kays, and sufficient police cover to guarantee an arrest both at Dane End and at Gates Garrage, were immense. Much of the operation had to be played by ear, and the police can justifiably claim that only by such resourcefulness were they able to spot the Volvo car that led to the Hoseins. Yet one is left with the feeling that, having convinced themselves Mrs. McKay was dead, their number one priority became the arrest of the abductors. If the one-in-a-thousand chance had come up, and Mrs. McKay had still been alive, what would have been her fate? The detectives had been told that if she appeared their one consideration was to be her safety. But if the kidnappers were cornered it was likely, from all their talk about telescopic rifles, that bullets were going to start flying; it was even possible that their first target would have been Mrs. McKay.

Finally there was the search at Rooks Farm, the most painstaking of its kind that the British police have ever carried out. Every possibility was considered and tested—except one. A number of pathologists have since commented on the failure of the Yard to call in one of their profession. Again it appears to have been a reluctance on the part of the authorities to experiment. Pathologists are presented with a body and asked to find the cause of death; here they would have had to work the other way round, testing samples taken from the farm for the presence of human remains. There was not much likelihood of success, but even that slight chance was not taken up.

If the British police are again faced with a kidnapping of the complexity of the McKay case, they will undoubtedly have to think out the moral issue of whether to allow negotiations to take place for the return of the victim; then, to avoid the publicity bogey, they must take the family and press fully into their confidence—and expect in return a period of complete silence. One important by-product of this would be to keep open the phone link to the victim's family. Had that happened in the McKay case who knows what might have been the outcome?

All these steps would need to be based on early diagnosis of the crime as a kidnapping. The sooner that has been decided, the quicker the publicity can be damped down. Again, had the police reached that conclusion, to the exclusion of all others, in the first forty-eight hours, there was an outside chance (admittedly a flimsy one) that the Hoseins might have been drawn into the open and their victim freed.

The Media

"Did publicity help to kill Mrs. McKay?" asked a newspaper headline after the Hoseins had been tried. The police are convinced that at the least it did little good; at the worst it may have hurried Mrs. McKay to her death.

Such a serious allegation deserves more attention than the press generally has paid to it. While the police have the sole responsibility for investigation and detection and, whatever their errors, are deemed to have acted from the best of motives, the same cannot always be said for the mass media. Here the underlying inference is that newspapers, television and radio, for various reasons—larger readerships or audiences, sensation, rivalry, or sheer irresponsibility or ignorance of their responsibilities—seriously impeded the police in their duty.

Three specific complaints against the media fall within the forty-eight hour "survival limit": the statement on the evening of 29th December which led police to discount the first ransom call; the publicity which blocked the telephone line to St. Mary House; and the publication of Mrs. McKay's first letter. On each of these issues, there is a direct conflict of views; even today police, press, and the McKays hold widely differing opinions about the responsibility for these critical situations.

The police maintain they had no chance of controlling the flow of information from St. Mary House on the night that Mrs. McKay disappeared, that the harm was done by those at the house who released the story to the Press Association and the *Sun* without police permission. Here there is a divergence of opinion among the police, the McKays, and Larry Lamb, the *Sun* editor, about who authorised the statement and what it was to contain. It seems, however, that Lamb is correct when he says he agreed on a statement for the papers with a detective at the house around ten o'clock that evening.

Lamb was subsequently to be accused not only of triggering

off the press interest but of using the family's connections with the News of the World Organisation to gain special treatment for the *Sun,* a member of that group. Lamb refutes this absolutely. "We were always at great pains not to take advantage of our special relationship. I put out a memo to the staff saying that the story had to be treated like any news story. They were only to use information that came over P.A. or that was supplied in the normal way by our police contacts."

The next plank in the police case against the media is that by a few minutes past one on the morning following Mrs. McKay's disappearance, hundreds of Fleet Street and BBC workers knew about it, and that this outside knowledge of the mystery caused the detectives to ignore the 1:15 A.M. ransom call: it could just have been somebody in the industry fooling about. Admittedly the papers were carrying Mrs. McKay's name; but the radio broadcast of the news at 1 A.M. was considered more significant by the police because of its proximity in time to the phone call. Yet that short BBC news item did not mention Mrs. McKay. There was just not enough time between one and 1:15 for anybody who had heard the news to discover who it referred to *and* find the number.

The various channels of news had certainly stirred up enormous interest in Mrs. McKay's fate as early as the morning of 30th December. By phone and letter to the house and the police station the messages came: some wanting to help, some to sympathise, some with crack-pot theories and some with sheer malicious intent. But worst of all, the police maintain, there was the endless stream of enquires from the journalists themselves. Eventually the family were advised to make no comment whatever ("Say one word to a journalist and he'll always have another question ready," they were told), and refer them to Wimbledon police station instead.

Only the police know just how much futile effort they were put to by the press's stimulating false leads, and only the police can surmise how seriously the Hoseins were hindered by the busy signal in their attempts to get through to Alick McKay in those early days. They say that on both counts the writers and broadcasters were irresponsible; the Fourth Estate can only plead that it was not aware of the gravity of its actions and that if the police wanted silence they should have taken Fleet Street into their confidence.

When Guiver and Smith decided not to release for publication the letter from Mrs. McKay telling her husband of her plight, it was not for reasons of security. The letter told them nothing apart from the fact that she was a prisoner and in a distraught state. Their motives were to save the family the distress of seeing this highly personal document circulated throughout the land. One can understand Smith's fury when he found that despite his efforts every word of the letter had leaked out. Both Smith and Guiver are in no doubt that it was someone from St. Mary House who released the text of this letter, despite their agreement with the occupants earlier that day to keep it secret. But Larry Lamb says categorically that the McKays and he kept to the agreement. He says that only when the *Sun* night news-staff saw the contents of the letter on the Press Association wires that evening did they feel they had no option but to follow suit.

So the blame goes round and round: Did the publicity, as Guiver suggests, drive the kidnappers to the point of no return? If one accepts the view of the experts in these matters, the FBI, it probably did. But then how was the press to know unless the Yard warned it of the consequences of its action? Which comes first, the press chicken or the Yard egg?

Lamb and other journalists have maintained that if the case was hindered by publicity, the publicity was put out to certain reporters by unofficial police sources. That is not a crime—although it may be a matter for police discipline— but it is an explanation, if not a justification, of the excess of zeal shown by the media. Some stories which appeared showed complete irresponsibility; others, after the crucial 30th December–1st January period were excellent examples of journalistic opportunism.

Several times stories appeared which the Commissioner, Sir John Waldron, felt might hinder the enquiry. Each time, at his request, papers showed their sense of responsibility by removing, or not carrying, the offending article. If there is a lesson in all this for the police, it is that they can trust newspapers and television to behave responsibly if they are taken into the authorities' confidence.

There is an important precedent for this. At the height of the world-wide protests against the war in Vietnam, a mass march was planned to the American Embassy in Grosvenor Square, London; it became famous as the 27th October, 1968, "demo." The press build-up to the march painted pictures of a bloody confrontation between protesters and police; it began to sound as if Grosvenor Square would become another Peterloo Massacre.

Then the Police Commissioner called all editors to his office for a briefing. Over sherry and savoury biscuits he gave them a complete run-down of what the police were expecting and what measures they were taking. On the basis of that information, the press was later able to give a less apprehensive resumé: Fleet Street, television, and radio did much to defuse the atmosphere of tension and the demonstration passed off with comparatively few incidents.

At a very late stage in the McKay case, Scotland Yard did consider whether it should again call editors together, explain the full background of the investigation in confidence, and ask the news media to impose a voluntary ban on further reports until the kidnappers were caught. But in the end it was decided that this would not really help the police: by that time most of the damage had already been done. Scotland Yard is to-day prepared to recognise that if the news media had been taken into its confidence at the very start, much of the publicity trouble could have been avoided.

But again, the delay in forming the proper view of Mrs. McKay's disappearance was the basis of the problem. If, on 30th December, editors had been called together and asked to impose a moratorium on reports of the case, and Mrs. McKay had then turned up alive, Scotland Yard would have looked rather silly in the eyes of Fleet Street and the whole idea of seeking press co-operation in this manner would have been irrevocably harmed. (That is Scotland Yard's view: again the police appear to be unduly sensitive of their image, a consideration that at times appeared to overshadow the only real priority, Mrs. McKay's safe return.)

In all their criticism of the communications industry, the police appear also to have overlooked the fact that in most "missing person" cases, publicity is of constructive value. A picture, a description, details of where the lost man, woman or child may be heading—these are routine matters the press is happy to print as part of what it regards as its public duty.

But in general the detectives, after the experience of the McKay case where their job was certainly made no easier by the newspaper interest, understandably feel that some curb should be applied to press and television activities in the event of another kidnapping. One does not need to agree with the case for police control of newspaper articles to appreciate the detectives' chagrin and bewilderment. So often it seemed that precisely the piece of information that needed to be kept secret for Mrs. McKay's good was being blazed over every newspaper and television screen: the first letter, the ransom drop fiasco at Dane End, the search of Rooks Farm.

While the situation was extremely grim in the first week, the job of trying to hold the ring was given to the Yard's Press Bureau. But the Bureau has no control over what is printed; furthermore, it does not have the complete support either of the detective or of the journalist. One senior policeman, not speaking specifically of the McKay case, said of the Bureau, "Often I've had to fight the Bureau to prevent them getting stuff I knew but didn't want to get out. They are often a hindrance to us."

That man believed the Press Bureau was too much on the side of the journalists. That is certainly not the view of Fleet Street. A member of the Crime Reporters' Association said of the Bureau, "They are always too busy defending the police or trying to act as their own censors. If the Yard had its way, there wouldn't be any crime reporters: just stool-pigeons down at the Bureau, feeding on bulletins from the official sources."

Commander Guiver would like to see the Press Bureau personnel replaced by senior policemen who would give background briefings on the lines of the Parliamentary lobby, backed by the power to control what was said or written about an investigation in progress. "Censorship? No, how can it be? The detective's motives are quite clear. A crime has to be solved and if certain stories are going to hinder the detection and conviction of the criminal, what justification can there be for allowing them to appear in print?"

Guiver's idea of a police lobby system in return for the power to vet crime articles would gain few supporters in Fleet Street, or in Parliament for that matter. The Parliamentary lobby, while probably the best system in the circumstances, is often abused by an M.P. or a Government minister who uses it to "float" a personal hobby-horse or to test in anonymity public reaction to an idea that he does not yet wish his name associated with. The journalist too is acutely aware of how officialdom can use its power of censorship to hide its own shortcomings. To give the police this power might assist an unscrupulous or inefficient policeman to strike out his mistakes with the censor's blue pencil.

That is the press argument. A policeman who sees crime booming because television shows the right way of opening a safe, or because a newspaper pays thousands of pounds to a notorious criminal for his memoirs, might claim that journalism has two faces—one of integrity and the other of hard-headed commercialism. He might interpret its concern for freedom of speech as fear over circulation or viewing figures.

It was one of the less wholesome features of the McKay case that at times the kidnapping itself was almost overshadowed by the in-fighting between press and police. The case has shown that it is certainly time the relationships between the two bodies were thoroughly re-examined. The police must be prepared to put more trust in press, television, and radio: the media must be prepared not to exploit that increased trust for its own ends.

The Family

Were the members of the family their own worst enemies? In their frenzy to save their mother, did they only make matters worse by enlisting the aid of the press and by getting in the way of the police?

Commander Guiver, who at times did not agree with what the McKays were doing, said, "To argue that the publicity may have hindered us is in no sense a criticism of any individual member of the family. The dilemma that faced Mr. McKay, a devoted family man, cannot fully be appreciated by anyone."

What the McKays had done in fact was only what would be expected of any family in such circumstances. At the very outset of the affair Alick McKay realized perhaps more than anyone, including the police, how vital time was. He may have guessed that his wife, violently torn from the serenity of life at St. Mary House at the coldest time of the year, was not going to be able to stand up to the rigours of captivity very long. When he and other members of his family and intimate circle of friends found the police maintaining a stolidly open mind on the case instead of accepting that it was a kidnapping, it is hardly to be wondered that they turned to their own devices. Alick and his associates in the News of the World Organisation were men who knew the power of publicity and how to harness it. They genuinely believed it was the way to get Muriel back alive. That they failed is not necessarily proof that their theory was wrong; after all, they might argue, the police were no more successful. The worst part of a kidnapping case for any family is the waiting and not knowing. The McKays were by nature leaders rather than led, used to making decisions upon which others should act. To expect them in these circumstances to sit back and do nothing was to demand the impossible.

One can understand the embarrassment of the police at the use of clairvoyants, just as one appreciates the willingness of the McKays to turn to anyone who offered hope. As David Dyer said at the time, "We are living on crumbs. . . ."

Every step the family took was from the highest of motives, as nobody, police or press, has ever disputed. If at times their actions appeared to impede the police, it was not surprising that the two parties did not always see eye to eye. The McKays wanted their mother back, and to them M3 was merely the vehicle through which she could be recovered. The police believed that the way to Mrs. McKay's recovery lay in first apprehending M3. The difference of emphasis was, of course, governed by their different outlooks: the McKays emotional, because of their love and concern for their mother; the police professional and calculating, because they could not afford to let emotion interfere with their task.

One detective, asked if he thought the police had made their first target the apprehension of the Hoseins to the detriment of Mrs. McKay, said, "I think they had to find these men before they could find her. After all, you were dealing with an alien culture here, one that does not think as we do."

Though Guiver and Smith had their suspicions—the idea that "four Jamaicans" were responsible enters the enquiry at an early stage—it was not until the door of Rooks Farm opened on 6th February that the police were aware that they had been up against this so-called "alien culture." For that matter, were the Hoseins "inscrutable, incomprehensible foreigners"? Arthur had lived in Britain for many years and was more British than Trinidadian in his way of life. Happily the issue of race was something that never raised its head during the enquiry or the trial, apart from Arthur's ravings at the judge from the dock. Had that too become an element in the story, life would have become almost intolerable for the police, for whom the racial problem is full of pitfalls.

By the mid-way stage in the enquiry, a complete rapprochement had been achieved between the police and the McKays, with Chief Superintendent Smith and Ian McKay the "intermediaries." By the week-end of 10th January, Alick McKay and Smith had reached an agreement under which, in exchange for a final man-to-man plea to the kidnappers on television and in the papers, the husband would thereafter impose a ban on further family publicity. This in itself was an immense concession on Alick's part: he still trusted the power of the news media, but he equally respected Smith's professionalism. From then on, Scotland Yard issued orders to its detectives and to the Press Bureau that they were in no way to encourage publicity. All enquiries from press and television were to be played down. This, the authorities believed, was the only way now of reaching the kidnappers. Against their own better judgement, the McKays followed suit.

One suspects that particularly after they had been warned their mother was probably dead, the family must have felt like saying to the police, "Please, take your tape-recorder and your notebooks and your questions and go away. Leave us alone. Don't think we don't appreciate your efforts, but we just want to be left in peace." Instead, they continued to play the supporting role to the detectives: feeding, grooming, advising, cheering, and consoling. For a family who had wandered into a war which was not of their choosing, the McKays were no mean fighters.

EPILOGUE

TIFFANYS IS a Wimbledon night club only a mile or two from Arthur Road, with a small dance floor and a South Sea Island decor. It has been the venue of many different types of celebration in its time, but none quite as macabre as the one held on the night of 12th October, 1970. The hosts were the Wimbledon police and the occasion was the previous week's successful prosecution of Arthur and Nizam Hosein at the Old Bailey.

Murder investigations tend to build up a strong *esprit de corps* among the participants, and it is quite customary for the detectives to hold a small celebration afterwards, usually in a pub. But because of the great number of people involved in the McKay case, the event began to take on the proportions of a mammoth office Christmas party. Twenty mini-skirted girls arrived, most of them from the administrative department at Scotland Yard. And so many guests were invited from Hertfordshire that a special coach had to be hired to transport them all. The club was closed to the public for the evening, and the festivities got under way soon after eight o'clock. Invitations were sent out to journalists, photographers, policemen, and a number of civilians, including a handful of publicans from both Stocking Pelham and Wimbledon. There was no sign of any of the McKays.

Drinks were laid out on a long table at the end of the room; after two hours, they ran out and there was a hasty collection so that more could be bought. Among the senior policemen present were Smith, Minors, and Harvey, head of the Hertfordshire CID. After a short "thank you" speech from Smith, couples danced to piped Muzak while others swapped reminiscences. Few people left for home until after midnight.

One of the subjects discussed at length during the party was the possibility of designing a special tie for all those who had been involved with the McKay case—another fairly common practice in Britain after a successful murder hunt. On this occasion a number of pressmen and police officers got as far as agreeing on a design. The tie was to be made of blue terylene embossed with gold crests consisting of two crossed bill-hooks with a rook sitting above them. One man was given the responsibility of taking the design to a tie maker and having a limited number made up. But, as it turned out, the idea never came to fruition.

Once the Hoseins had been arrested, St. Mary House was put up for sale. It was bought by Howard Baverstock, a wealthy local furniture manufacturer and friend of the McKays, who paid over £30,000 for it. Alick left Wimbledon for good and moved to a flat in Central London.

On 17th November, 1970 there was a last-minute reprieve from the RAF for the Hoseins' two ferocious alsatians, Rex and Reggie, who were due to be destroyed on the following day. Instead they were taken to RAF Debden, a police-dog training establishment in Essex.

Rooks Farm and its contents were auctioned on Wednesday, 18th November. The auction, held in a crowded marquee beside the house, was attended by more than 250 people, including Detective Inspector Minors and a small group of Wimbledon detectives. Earlier, the farm had been opened for the first time to sightseers, who filed curiously through the rooms and the various outbuildings. Only one room remained locked throughout the day: Arthur Hosein's tailoring shop, complete with flat irons, sewing machines, and a long workbench.

Bidding for the farm began at £5,000, and within ninety seconds it had been sold for £18,500 to Mrs. Arthur Lilley, wife of a Hertfordshire caravan dealer. Asked if living in a house with such bizarre associations would frighten her, Mrs. Lilley was emphatic: "Good gracious no; it won't frighten me at all." The auctioneers, G. E. Sworder of Bishop's Stortford, also sold off most of the possessions on the farm, including the dark blue Volvo saloon. But the first sale of the farm was never completed. In June, 1971, it was again sold by auction to an undisclosed buyer.

The day following the Rooks Farm auction saw the beginning of a complicated legal wrangle between Arthur Hosein and his wife Else. Arthur had instructed that all the proceeds from the sale should go back to his parents in Trinidad. But on Wednesday, 19th November, Mrs. Hosein obtained an emergency injunction from the Divorce Court registrar at Somerset House restraining her husband from disposing of half the proceeds of the sale.

A week later, Mrs. Hosein filed a divorce petition claiming cruelty. In a sworn statement, she said that when she had visited her husband in Leicester prison, he had accused her of having a good time while he was in custody. "He told me that I would not get a penny, that I could go to hell and that the proceeds were to go to his father, who would take them back to Trinidad," she added.

On 2nd December, Arthur was driven from prison to the Divorce Court under a heavy police guard. For most of his time in court, he was handcuffed to a pair of burly police officers. He told the judge that his only care was the welfare of his two children. He was then asked why he was not represented by counsel. "I do not have confidence in the legal profession, and decided to take on the case myself," he replied, showing no loss of his old cocksureness. During the hearing, he laughingly acknowledged the judge's remark that he would probably not be in a position to earn money "for a long time." He agreed to the judge's making an order to freeze the £10,000 proceeds from Rooks Farm until the hearing of the divorce action brought by his wife.

Although Alick McKay's courage has impressed all who have come into contact with him since the murder, there are still times when he is obviously lost in personal grief. Colleagues at the *News of the World* noticed that on the first anniversary of his wife's disappearance he was "distinctly off-colour and not himself."

At his home in Utrecht Gerard Croiset, the Dutch clairvoyant, keeps a large file on the McKay case and a tape-recorded account of all his dealings with David Dyer and Eric Cutler. As a result of his experiences during his visit to England, he has vowed to stay firmly put at home in future. "I shall not go abroad again," he says. "I can do without all the publicity, it only gives me extraneous impressions which get in the way. I'm sure I can be of more help working from here."

On 3rd January, 1971, reports appeared in some British newspapers claiming that both Arthur Hosein and his brother had, on separate occasions, been beaten up by fellow prisoners trying to discover the whereabouts of Mrs. McKay's body. The Home Office admitted that Arthur had received a black eye in a scuffle with another prisoner, but denied that any violence had been done to Nizam.

The *Sun* continued to entertain and outrage. First condemned by the Press Council for printing the memoirs of train robber Ronald Biggs in January 1971, it was later named "Newspaper of the Year" in Granada Television's influential "What The Papers Say" awards. Among the qualities cited were "its rapid increase in circulation, its admirable writers, and wide variety in reader appeal." A month later, the *Sun's* circulation passed the two million mark.

On 3rd October, 1969, after his grilling from David Frost about the Christine Keeler memoirs, Rupert Murdoch had stormed out of the London Weekend Television studios and

told reporters, "London Weekend Television has made an important enemy."

By February 1971, with typical panache, Murdoch had gained a large shareholding in the company and was in the process of turning it upside-down. In the month after he became executive controller, LWT lost seven of its senior executives.

Murdoch's swift move into British commercial television (he already had extensive radio and TV interests in Australia) had begun in November 1970 when G.E.C. Ltd., the giant electrical group, transferred its 7½ per cent voting interest in London Weekend to the *News of the World*. Despite the Independent Television Authority's traditional hostility towards newspaper proprietors, Murdoch took Sir Arnold Weinstock's place on the company board and a month later injected £505,000 into LWT's sagging finances.

But at the end of February, 1971, the ITA intervened. At that time, the Authority considered the position of LWT and Mr. Murdoch, who had effectively gained executive control of the company. ITA instructed the television company to appoint a new managing director and a new programme controller. As a result, Mr. John Freeman, former British ambassador in Washington, was appointed chief executive and managing director, and Mr. Cyril Bennett returned to his previous job as programme controller. For once, it seemed, Mr. Murdoch had met his match.

Scotland Yard never published the cost of the police operation in the McKay case; it is doubtful whether it was ever specifically costed. Many of the expenses were fixed: police salaries, expenditure on vehicles, telephone and telex communications. But at the height of the enquiry, wages alone were running at about £3,000 a week. Incidental expenses, whether taken as time off for extra hours worked or paid in cash, amounted to almost another £1,000 a week. On top of that, there was the work done by civilan staff and by police in other forces and abroad. In all, solving the McKay mystery must have cost the police—and the public—in the region of £30,000 or £40,000.

After the divorce court hearing, Else and Arthur Hosein

reached an amicable agreement over property and Mrs. Hosein visited her husband in prison at his own request. Among the things Arthur had asked for was a bird cage. "He told me that he was going to breed budgerigars," Mrs. Hosein said. "He has always liked birds and says he's interested in training them."